# Michael Jordan
*and the*
# New
# Global Capitalism

# Michael Jordan

## and the
# New
# Global Capitalism

Walter LaFeber

*To Walter + Janet —*
*With Best Wishes —*
*Walter LaFeber*
*11/6/99*

W. W. NORTON & COMPANY
*New York • London*

For information about permission to reproduce
selections from this book, write to Permissions,
W. W. Norton & Company, Inc., 500 Fifth Avenue,
New York, NY 10110

The text of this book is composed in Garth Graphic
with the display set in Runic Condensed.
Composition by Allentown Digital Services Division
of R.R. Donnelley & Sons Company.
Manufacturing by the Haddon Craftsmen.
Book design by Charlotte Staub


**Library of Congress Cataloging-in-Publication Data**

LaFeber, Walter.
    Michael Jordan and the new global capitalism /
by Walter LaFeber.
        p.   cm.
    Includes bibliographical references and index.
    **ISBN 0-393-04747-4**
    1. Jordan, Michael, 1963–   .  2. Basketball
players—United States—Biography.   3. Sports—
Marketing.   4. International business enterprises.
5. Nike (Firm).   I. Title.
GV884.J67L34   1999
796.323'092—dc21
[b]      98-55910      CIP


W. W. Norton & Company, Inc., 500 Fifth Avenue,
New York, N.Y. 10110
www.wwnorton.com

W. W. Norton & Company Ltd., 10 Coptic Street,
London WC1A 1PU

1 2 3 4 5 6 7 8 9 0

*This book is for*
**Matthew and Trevor Kahl**

# Contents

*"You have spoken in jest about New York as the Capital of Culture but in 25 years it will be just as London is now. Culture follows money and all the refinements of aestheticism can't stave off its change of seat.... We will be the Romans in the next generations as the English are now."*

F. SCOTT FITZGERALD to Edmund Wilson, 1921

*"Now the experience of sports is everywhere. It's all-encompassing, and instantaneous. It's right there beside you from cradle to grave... the culture of the world."*

PHIL KNIGHT,
founder and Chief Executive Officer of Nike,
as quoted in Donald Katz, *Just Do It: The Nike Spirit in the Corporate World* (New York, 1994)

"We can have a market economy, but we cannot have a market society."

GEORGE SOROS, 1998

# Preface

This is a short book on some large subjects. It argues that the world changed fundamentally in the 1970s and early 1980s. In this sense, the twenty-first century began during those years, for powerful forces that will shape the early part of the new century significantly appeared for the first time. Or, to rephrase, a new era did not begin with the end of the Cold War and the collapse of the Soviet Union between 1989 and 1991, but with the information revolution, the new power of U.S. capital and transnational corporations to drive that revolution, and the reaction—sometimes violent—in the United States and abroad to that revolution. This new era has been called "the information age," and described as "post-industrial," "post-modern," and even "post-imperialist" or "late capitalist." Whatever it is termed, it marks the beginning of something different in world history.[1]

At its end, this book briefly speculates on the meaning of the story in the long history of imperialism, including the rise of what has come to be known as cultural imperialism. It also touches on the question of whether U.S. exploitation of the new information age, so well exemplified by Michael Jordan's successes, will lead to a better twenty-first century or, as some believe, a bloody clash of cultures and civilizations.

The analysis uses the sport of basketball to begin examining these subjects. Why basketball? Because with the help of new media the marketing of basketball has become an important fixture in global as well as American culture. Because some of the pioneering transnational corporations are exploiting American sports so profitably and with far-reaching social consequences. Because basketball has attracted both women and men as players as well as spectators since the game first appeared in 1891. And because basketball produced Michael Jordan.

This account assumes that the importance of U.S. foreign relations diminished not at all with the Cold War's end after 1989. The nation's overseas influence and power has only become more fascinating—contrary to what some of the more parochial members of the U.S. Congress, some academic departments, and a few publishing houses may believe—and it has become vastly more important for new generations of Americans to understand this.

Just how far that influence reached became clear to Max Perelman, a young American college student, when he traveled through remote regions of China in January 1997. While stranded by winter weather in west Sichuan, a long fifteen hundred miles from Beijing, he encountered a group of Tibetans bound for their capital, Lhasa. The Tibetans, Perelman recalled, had never strayed far from their native village. They had apparently not seen anything like his camera. As they shared with him bites of meat from the raw, bloody, rib cage of an unspecified animal retrieved from their rucksacks, the group began to discuss things American. Just how, one of the Tibetans asked the young American, was Michael Jordan doing?

How these travelers knew about the Chicago Bulls' star was never made clear. That they knew about him, however, was perhaps not surprising. He was the most famous athlete and one of the most recognizable people in the world. Jordan and his "Red Oxen," as his team was known in much of Asia, had gained renown for their basketball championships. But Jordan was especially famous for another reason: he was the superhuman who flew through the air in television advertisements as he endlessly and effortlessly dunked basketballs and, simultaneously, sold Nike sneakers. These glamorous advertisements flew about the globe thanks to new technologies such as earth satellites and cable. This communication revolution conveniently appeared for global commercial use just as Jordan was beginning a spectacular basketball career in the 1980s, and as Phil Knight was building Nike into a mighty multibillion-dollar transnational empire that ingeniously marketed its sneakers over the new media. Jordan's fame rose to the point that at the 1992 Olympic games he was embarrassed by being asked at a press conference if he were a "god." But as *Time* magazine noted, "If Michael Jordan is God, then Phil Knight put him in heaven."[2]

Much of this post-1970s technology was dominated by U.S. empire-builders, notably the flamboyant Ted Turner. He had sunk the family fortune into the emerging business of cable television and communication satellites, only to go nearly bankrupt in the early 1980s. Not long after, however, he built CNN (Cable News Network) into an international as well as American powerhouse. Indeed, the network became so international that Turner outlawed the use of the word "foreign" in its broadcasts. Nothing was foreign to CNN. In 1997, Turner stunned the world by giving one billion dollars over a ten-year period to the United Nations to help its international humanitarian programs. It stood to reason that he gave this incredible gift to the UN instead of to, say, his home city of Atlanta, Georgia. CNN, like Nike and Michael Jordan, had burst beyond mere city boundaries to become a global institution—and had grown rich by moving far beyond U.S. borders to create a worldwide marketplace.

Jordan's role in this growing Americanization of global media was profound. As noted in the following chapters, he became a part of the heated argument over whether African-American athletes increasingly dominated basketball and many other sports because they were physically different from and superior to whites, or because they concentrated on these sports due to racism since other careers were closed to them. And eventually, Jordan became a figure who often transcended race. Black social critic Stanley Crouch observed that "in 1960, if white girls in the suburbs had had posters of a Negro that dark on the wall, there would have been hell to pay. That kind of racial paranoia is not true of the country now. Today you have girls who are Michael Jordan fanatics, and their parents don't care."[3]

The immense success of Jordan and the National Basketball Association (NBA) has also helped shape the role of women in professional sports. The combination of talented and imaginative female athletes who appeared in the 1970s and 1980s, simultaneously with the growing popularity of basketball created by NBA marketing techniques and new media coverage, has led to the creation of professional women's leagues and lucrative endorsement contracts for a few of their stars. As noted in chapter 1, women were playing basketball within weeks after the game was invented in 1891. In 1973 the U.S. government passed Title IX, a historic step that required equal facilities for men's and women's sports at institutions receiving federal funds.

As is also noted below, basketball has always been a

commercial product. In the 1980s its ability to churn out profits reached a new level with the appearance of revolutionary technology and imaginative entrepreneurs (including David Stern, the commissioner of the NBA), who were determined to exploit it. Jordan became a world icon, even in far-off Sichuan, in part because the number of television sets for every hundred people around the globe doubled to 23.4 between 1981 and 1997.[4]

While the new media could create fame and fortunes in world markets for Jordan and Nike's Phil Knight, so too could that media expose their errors, tragedies, and embarrassments globally. A "Faustian bargain" emerged in which celebrities such as Jordan sold themselves via the media, and ambitious companies such as Nike likewise sold their goods. But, in return, the media blazed Jordan's personal misfortunes across the world's television screens and told billions of viewers about Nike's subcontractors in Asia who exploited and sexually abused the workers who made the sneakers. Jordan was often asked to take stands on these and other difficult political issues. On the whole, he declined. Critics, even admirers, charged that he cared more about retaining his commercial appeal than dealing with the most important issues of the day. Taking a stand could alienate some of the potential buyers of the goods he endorsed.

Jordan's career also helps us understand something about the nature of U.S. power in the post–Cold-War era. Phil Knight liked to say that by the 1990s sports had become the world's most important entertainment. No one better exemplified the power of that entertainment than Jordan and Knight. American popular culture (the jazz of Duke Ellington, the musical theatre of George Gershwin, the dance of Fred Astaire and Martha Graham, blue jeans, McDonald's fast food, Coca-Cola), has long been part of U.S. influence and profit overseas. The power of that popular culture, however, multiplied with the technological marvels that appeared in the 1960s and 1970s.

In earlier eras, a culture was transmitted across national boundaries by migration, travel, or reading. Since leisure travel and literacy were often limited to the rich, the understanding—and exploitation—of other cultures was often enjoyed only by elites. Television and the post-1970s media, along with cheaper and more rapid transportation via jet airplanes, changed all that. Culture could move with nearly the speed of sound and reach billions of people, not just the privileged. Jordan and Nike (and McDonald's and Disney), suddenly enjoyed the power to reach vast audiences with an efficiency unimagined several generations earlier.

Jordan and Nike, moreover, exploited yet another kind of power new to the post-1970s media. For centuries, the control over mass dispersal of information was held in the hands of monarchs, the Church, or, more recently, powerful newspaper and radio owners. After the 1970s, however, this power to spread information and culture became more decentralized. Masses of people could pass on information in large globs over computer systems. When only three major U.S. television networks existed, as in the 1950s, the network owners generally controlled what people could see. With 70, 150, or even 500 channels, audiences enjoyed much wider choices. Thus Jordan and Nike could select certain channels (MTV) to target young buyers of sneakers, or use other channels (ESPN) watched by sports fans. And with the emergence of globe-girdling communication-satellite systems to carry these television advertisements, Jordan and Knight instantaneously flashed their messages, and themselves, around the world.[5]

It was an awesome power. Transnational corporations not only played a dominant role in creating and defining American popular culture, but they used that culture's own seductiveness to influence the language, eating habits, clothes, and television watching of peoples around the earth. " 'Globalization,' " John Cassidy wrote, "is the buzzword of the late twentieth century," and it is powered by vast amounts of capital—and by "English, the global language of money." Cassidy believed that "Globalization is set to become the biggest political issue of the next century." It already had become an interesting issue, for example, in the former British West Indies, where basketball began to displace cricket as the national sport, especially on islands where television was most watched. On Trinidad and Tobago, the black lower class took over basketball and turned it into a statement for their class and racial pride. Their model, historian Allen Guttmann noted, was the NBA, as they adopted NBA team and player names, while mimicking moves of the players. Thus the sports of the British Empire gave way to the technology of the American Century.[6]

Other peoples have not as willingly accepted U.S. influence. A respected historian (and former basketball coach), in Canada, Geoffrey Smith, likened the new era to the corrupt, rampant exploitation of the so-called Gilded Age in the United States of the 1870s–1890s. In the States, Smith argued, there has developed a "new Gilded Age—with its accompanying greed and rapacity." Among its worse qualities is that "the 'market' in sport defines nearly everything." The immense amount of money and celebrity generated by sports, he concluded, leads many, especially the young, to conclude that playing games is more important than education and politics.[7]

Smith's and other Canadians' concern about U.S. influence is understandable. American television programs became so popular that by the mid-1990s the Canadian government finally required television and radio stations to broadcast a minimum amount of programming from Canadians themselves. Some 96 percent of films shown in Canada were foreign-made, the large majority from Hollywood. Four of five magazines sold were foreign, mostly American. But the Canadians were hardly alone. Other friends and allies of the United States also warned that its power was unwelcome. "The United States has assets not yet at the disposal of any other power," French Foreign Minister Hubert Vedrine declared in 1997. These assets included "political influence, the supremacy of the dollar, control of the communications networks, 'dream factories' [that is, Hollywood and television], new technologies. . . . The situation is virtually unprecedented." Vedrine argued that France had to ensure Americans did not fall into the temptation of "unilateralism and the risk of hegemony" over other peoples.[8]

Even in Germany, staunch U.S. Cold-War ally, a leading newsmagazine, *Der Spiegel,* warned in 1997: "Never before in modern history has a country dominated the earth so totally as the United States does today. . . . The Americans are acting, in the absence of limits put to them by anybody or anything, as if they own a blank check in their 'McWorld.' " It was time, *Der Spiegel* suggested, to fight back before the entire world "wears a 'Made in USA' label."[9]

Growing resistence to the power of American popular culture led to an intense debate over whether the United States was actually an imperialist spreading its culture so effectively that it was radically changing, if not potentially destroying, other cultures. Some of these observers believed that Americans fooled themselves if they thought other peoples would change their traditional way of living just to enjoy U.S. products. Indeed, some argued that as Americans went abroad to spread their culture and fatten their pocketbooks, they would instead have to change their own culture. That is, they would have to become less nationalistic, less ignorant of and more open to other cultures and religions.

The new global commercial power exemplified by Michael Jordan, Nike, CNN, in other words, is making Americans fear that as they are electronically interspersed into the world community, they are threatened by the loss of their national identity—they are a people becoming too "multicultural" and sympathetic to the global power of groups like the United Nations—just as other peoples begin to eat and dress like Americans. Such fear moved into American political and economic debates during the 1990s, especially through the surprising number of votes given to Pat Buchanan and Ross Perot, who attacked such outside influences. As revolutionary technology thus integrated Americans into the rest of the world, many of them feared the strangeness and challenges that they encountered. Americans had feared the strangeness and challenges of other peoples since the seventeenth century, but never before had such dangers been so instantaneous, so immediate, as they were in the new, tightly wired world.[10]

In this developing battle of capital versus culture, capital will ultimately win. The United States is, and has been since World War I, the world's clearinghouse for capital. By the 1990s, the volume of that capital became overwhelming; some $1.5 trillion moved through New York City financial markets every *day.* This torrent of money developed the new media and powered the new transnational corporations. For good or ill, it wielded the power to bring other governments nearly to their knees during the recurring financial crises of the 1990s. It even forced the world's superpower, the U.S. government, to change social priorities and spending policies. Other nations, such as France and Japan, do not necessarily favor this kind of fundamental change and will certainly resist such power. American culture, if powered by vast sums of capital, will thus change as it becomes more global or else produce conflict that will have explosive results for U.S. politics and security.

The story of how the United States and the world reached this point begins in the 1890s, when the American economy first became the world's greatest, and when basketball was first invented. The history of basketball, especially in the era of Michael Jordan, helps us understand this era known as "the American Century."

The Asian economic downturn of 1998 stunningly exemplified the crises and challenges to U.S.-capital-driven culture that Americans (and many others) will face in the early twenty-first century. The dramatic decline in Asian economics touched off a near-panic globally: Russia teetered on the brink of bankruptcy, Brazil faced severe crisis, and even U.S. stock markets dropped sharply. The Asians, notably the Japanese, Indonesians, and Malaysians, blamed the West, especially U.S. capitalists, for overwhelming their economies, making quick profits, then exiting—leaving behind shattered societies. U.S. government and business officials, however, emphatically placed the blame on the Asians themselves for trying to close off and overly influence markets, often through a kind of "capitalist cronyism" that favored Asian over Western investors.

It was a clash of capitalisms and cultures of the most dramatic, and important, kind. Then it turned worse. Under tremendous U.S. pressure, 102 nations, led by Japan (the world's second largest economy), agreed to open their financial markets to foreign investors. Suddenly U.S. firms began buying up or controlling Asian firms that had long been protected from foreign influence. The most important American economic official, Alan Greenspan, Chairman of the Federal Reserve system, announced that these other nations were finally seeing the light; they were moving toward "the type of market system which we have in this country." A century of U.S. economic power apparently climaxed with an ultimate triumph. Others, however, were not so sure. Anti-American feelings rose in Japan, Malaysia, Indonesia, and elsewhere as these nations tried to protect themselves from U.S. capitalism's cultural backriders. Otherwise, as one American reporter wrote from Japan, it would only be a matter of time before an Asian family would take cash from their corner U.S. bank, "drive off to Walmart and fill the trunk of their Ford with the likes of Fritos and Snickers," then stop at the American-owned movie theater to see the latest Disney film before returning home to check their U.S. mutual fund accounts and America Online (on their IBM computer with Microsoft software).[11]

Asians see this as nothing less than the U.S. "desire to bury Asian values," and they are not pleased. Nor are many Americans. Former Secretary of State Henry Kissinger (later a wealthy business consultant with many ties to Asia) put it directly: "I am disturbed by the tendency to treat the Asian economic crisis as another opportunity to acquire control of Asian companies' assets cheaply and to reconstitute them on the American model. This is courting long-term disaster."[12]

At the center of this discussion arises one all-important question. Given Americans' increased dependence on world markets for jobs, given how the new technology is locking Americans into a sometimes violent global community that too easily resorts to terrorism to fight the United States, and given that Americans have no choice but to be participants in that complex, often threatening global community—what kind of participants will Americans be? They wield immense power, and unless that power is accompanied by an understanding of its effects and how it came to be, the twenty-first century will be a continuation of the confrontations and bloodshed of the twentieth century. But with new technologies the clashes will occur in a confined, interlinked global village from which no one can escape to safety.

On January 13, 1999, Jordan announced his retirement from basketball. The *Chicago Tribune* headlined, END OF AN ERA. "The most popular athlete in the world and undoubtedly the most popular in American sports history," experts gushed. "Beyond that he transcended the game, becoming an international celebrity and spokesman."[13]

The impact was indeed global. JORDAN RETIRES! SHOCK FELT AROUND THE WORLD, a Japanese sportspaper headlined. Basketball was a minor sport in Japan, but thanks to television ads, Air Jordan Nike sneakers had sold for as much as $1,000 a pair and some were collected like jewels. Mexican, Polish, German, Spanish, Chinese, and British headlines, among others, echoed Japanese feelings. Standing at the end of a century in which the United States had come to command global financial power, communications systems, marketing networks, and cutting-edge technologies, Jordan exemplified this imperial control—and also some of the explosively dangerous challenges and high costs Americans now confronted in the newly wired world's new century.[14]

Michael Jordan
*and the*
New
Global Capitalism

# CHAPTER I

## *A Century of Preparation*

At the end of the twentieth century, Americans, their economy, and their culture seemed to dominate many parts of the globe. A basketball player who lived in Chicago, Michael Jordan, was arguably the most recognized and revered of those Americans to billions of people worldwide. In China, schoolchildren ranked him with Zhou Enlai as the two greatest figures in twentieth-century history.[1] The children knew Zhou because he helped create their Communist Revolution. They knew Jordan because he miraculously floated through the air as both an athlete and as a pitchman for American-produced advertisements for Nike shoes, which the children avidly followed on television. His coach in Chicago, Phil Jackson, believed that Jordan "had somehow been transformed in the public mind from a great athlete to a sports deity"—especially when an amazed Jackson saw people kneeling before the statue of Jordan that stands in front of the United Center, home of the Chicago Bulls.[2]

Jordan's phenomenal athletic prowess was unquestioned. Indiana University basketball coach Bob Knight (known for his two national championships as well as his blunt style), told sports columnist Mike Lupica: "Michael Jordan is the best that will ever play this game." Sociologist Harry Edwards, an African American who blisteringly attacked professional sports and the roles assigned black players, declared: "If I were charged with introducing an alien life form to the epitome of human potential, creativity, perseverance, and spirit, I would introduce that alien life form to Michael Jordan."[3]

To Edwards and many others, Jordan personified not only the imaginative, individual skills that Americans dream of displaying in a society that adores graceful and successful individualism, but the all-out competitive spirit and discipline that Americans like to think drove their nation to the peak of world power. Coach Jackson phrased it directly: "Michael is a little bit of a shark. He's competitive to the extent that he'd like to beat you for your last cent and send you home without your clothes."[4]

Such skills quickly translated into money and power in the world of the late twentieth century. But Jordan was not just an athlete, he was an African-American athlete who earned $30 million a year for playing with the Bulls and twice that amount from his endorsements and personal businesses. Within his own lifetime, African-American athletes had been victimized and exploited—not made multimillionaires. They were also often condemned for choosing merely to dunk basketballs or catch footballs, rather than acting as role models for future doctors, lawyers, or business leaders. That Jordan became a hero for the many races in American society was thus somewhat surprising. That he could transform this role into becoming the most successful advertising figure in the world was historic. His success in good part can be traced back to his family and North Carolina background.

## The North Carolina Legacy

Since its founding in 1891, basketball has been dominated by players—African-American and white, male and female—who came from the playgrounds, YMCAs, YWCAs, and athletic clubs of America's cities. Michael Jordan, however, did not grow up in a large urban area. He was born on February 17, 1963, to parents living temporarily in Brooklyn, New York. James Jordan, a sharecropper's son, was attending a Brooklyn training school so he could pursue his ambition of becoming a supervisor at the General Electric plant outside the small town of Wallace, North Carolina. Deloris Jordan was meanwhile moving steadily up the corporate ladder at United Carolina Bank in Wallace.

Michael grew up in a close-knit middle-class family that revolved around the children's enthusiasms for baseball, football, track, and, to a lesser extent, basketball. He lived in a small town far removed from the violence then shaking much of the South as the nation painfully moved from enforced segregation, which had been in place since the 1890s, to enforced integration of the races. James and Deloris preached, "You just didn't judge people's color." And if ignorant, racist folks hurled insults, you just determined to "move on" rather than let it slow your climb up the middle-class ladder.[5]

In 1970, the Jordans did indeed move up to better jobs in the larger city of Wilmington, North Carolina. Again, they missed the worst of the civil-rights violence. Michael seldom encountered racial taunts, although he once ground a Popsicle into the hair of a girl who called him "nigger."[6] But Laney High School had been integrated before he arrived, and Jordan became a sports star—but only by his senior year. As a sophomore he was cut from the varsity basketball team. "I went to my room and I closed the door and I cried," he later told sportswriter Bob Greene. "For a while I couldn't stop. Even though there was no one else home at the time, I kept the door shut. It was important to me that no one hear me or see me." Nor could he get dates with girls because, as he recalled, he had an odd haircut and drew laughs for his habit of playing basketball with his tongue hanging out.[7]

Within months after being cut, Michael's world changed. In his junior year, he suddenly grew to 6´3˝. He arose at sunup to push his new body through special drills. This development came too late, however, to attract attention from many top colleges. His biographer, Jim Naughton, noted that Jordan was not even rated among the three hundred leading high-school prospects at the start of his senior year. He did enter a summer basketball camp in Pittsburgh where he played well against some of the nation's best young players and was named Most Valuable Player. His talent drew the attention of Roy Williams, an assistant to the legendary coach at the University of North Carolina, Dean Smith. (Williams later became famous in his own right as coach at the University of Kansas.) Michael had never cared for the state university, but his mother did—especially after Dean Smith visited and talked about the importance of education rather than the glories of basketball. Anyway, there were few other offers, and his sister Roslyn (who graduated after only three years of high school) was also going to Chapel Hill.

For twenty years, Dean Smith's system had been renowned for reaching, but never winning, national championship games. Smith produced superb professional players, employed tough discipline, insisted on nightly study halls, and held the belief that unproven freshmen should devote themselves more to books than to playing time. Jordan's defense and passing skills were weak, but his quickness and imagination on offense, as well as his fire and work ethic, forced Smith to start him alongside two All-Americans (and later pro stars), James Worthy and Sam Perkins. By midseason of his freshman year (1981–1982), North Carolina was ranked number one in the country. Jordan was a leading scorer.

At the end of his freshman season, he suddenly became a national figure. Jordan ignored a painful throat infection to lead his team to the Atlantic Coast Conference championship. Worthy, Perkins, and Jordan then took the Tar Heels through the NCAA Championship tournament until they met Georgetown and the Hoyas' 7´1˝ All-American, Patrick Ewing, in New Orleans before some 61,000 fans and a huge national television audience.

With 32 seconds to play, Georgetown led 62–61. Dean Smith was again on the verge of missing a national championship. Smith called a time-out and told the players to get the ball to Jordan for a final shot. Smith was trusting a freshman to make the decisive points. Jordan took a pass on the right side of the floor and shot. The ball swished through the net sixteen feet away. Smith had his championship. Worthy led the scoring with 28 points, but Jordan was the hero. North Carolina's assistant coach Eddie Fogler observed: "That kid doesn't even realize it yet, but he's part of history now. People will remember that shot 25 years from now."[8]

The nineteen-year-old thus became famous for grace, and success, under immense pressure. "I've seen other great athletes," Dean Smith later declared, "but Michael also has the intelligence, the court savvy . . . he was a hero so many times at the end of games—it was uncanny."[9] Jordan's professional coach, Phil Jackson, noted that in the many last-second situations from which Michael emerged the hero, "More often than not, he'll replay the last-second shot he took to win the 1982 NCAA championship. . . . [he] says to himself, 'Okay, I've been here before.' "[10]

After the triumph in New Orleans, Jordan's college career became anticlimactic, if successful. During his sophomore year, North Carolina failed to reach the NCAA finals, although sports journalists named Jordan College Player of the Year. In the summer of 1983, he led the U.S. Pan-American team to a gold medal in Venezuela, a trip that led him to choose cultural geography as his undergraduate major. In his junior year, the Tarheels again fell short of the NCAA finals. But Jordan had become, in the words of *Sports Illustrated*'s Curry Kirkpatrick, "the finest all-around amateur player in the world."[11]

In the spring of 1984, Jordan announced he would delay his senior year to turn professional. He had little left to prove in college. Deloris Jordan wanted her son to remain at Chapel Hill until he obtained a degree. James Jordan and, surprisingly, Dean Smith, sided with Michael. In the National Basketball Association's draft in June 1984, college's best all-around player was not the first pick. Or the second. With the first choice, the lowly Houston Rockets selected Hakeem Olajuwon. (A great center, Olajuwon led Houston to NBA championships in 1994 and 1995, the two years Jordan temporarily retired from the game.) Portland, with the second pick, took 7'1" Sam Bowie of Kentucky. Plagued with injuries, Bowie never became an NBA star.

Chicago, long a losing team, then selected Jordan. Bulls' General Manager Rod Thorn bluntly declared that he wanted a center, not a guard such as Jordan. "We wish he were 7 feet, but he isn't," Thorn griped. "There wasn't a center available. What can you do?" *Chicago Tribune* columnist Bernie Lincicome suggested that Thorn might count his blessings. Lincicome wrote sarcastically that

Thorn and the Bulls "had tried to avoid Jordan" and instead "got stuck with . . . maybe the greatest natural basketball talent, inch for inch, in this young decade." Lincicome noted that Jordan was also an attractive person with a sense of humor—which was fortunate because he "will need a few laughs to ease the shock of moving from a winning team at North Carolina to a loser in Chicago."[12]

Suspicion spread that the Bulls feigned unhappiness so they would not have to pay Jordan as much as he was worth. If so, he quickly destroyed that illusion when he signed a five-year contract for $800,000 annually. Thus Jordan and the Bulls began one of the most successful and profitable journeys in modern sports.

That happy journey could hardly be anticipated, however, in 1984. Jordan joined a deeply troubled professional league. Basketball was at a crossroads in the United States. Few people abroad seemed to care about the NBA at all, certainly not when it competed with soccer, hockey, or home teams in Europe for attention. Jordan and a new era of technology changed all that.

## The Naismith Legacy

Most major sports have obscure beginnings, but basketball's can be pinpointed in time and told in detail. Those are not its only unique qualities. No game became so popular and commercialized more rapidly.

James Naismith certainly did not set out to make his game ring cash registers. The Canadian-born teacher merely hoped to keep his job at Springfield College in Massachusetts after his superior, Dr. Luther Gulick, ordered him to do something to keep young men out of trouble between football and baseball seasons. The boys in the class were almost out of control; two of the school's instructors had flatly refused to face them. Because it was

Massachusetts, any new winter game would best be played indoors. Because Springfield College was a training school for the worldwide missionary activities of the Young Men's Christian Association (YMCA), Naismith's answer would have to deal with the "mind, and soul" (as Gulick put it), as well as the body and especially adrenaline of each student.

Naismith first tried variations of football and lacrosse indoors, but these quickly got out of hand. Desperate, he began writing rules for a new game. There was to be no striking or running with the ball (as in lacrosse). The ball was instead to be passed. Nine players were on each side because Naismith's class had eighteen students. (Five on each side became the rule in 1897.) The goal was placed high above the players so they would not as easily fight each other as they would around a ground-level goal. The goals, peach baskets from a nearby orchard, were placed ten feet high (where they have forever remained), because this happened to be the height of the gymnasium's balcony to which Naismith could most easily attach the baskets.

How new was his sport can be debated. Historians have discovered that for two thousand years the Mayas and Aztecs played a game in which a large ball was to be passed through a ring at the two ends of the court. The losing team's leader was sometimes sacrificed to the gods. In Naismith's home country, the Abnaki of eastern Canada tried to keep an air-filled ball aloft. But no evidence has been found that Naismith knew about these earlier sports.[13]

Named by one of Naismith's first players as Basket Ball (it finally became one word in 1921), the sport's popularity rapidly spread. Within the first week after Naismith introduced the game, audiences collected to watch the play. The shouts attracted female teachers who quickly taught the game to young women. Within three months after basketball appeared, a women's tournament was held. In 1893, the first women's intercollegiate game took place at Smith College in Massachusetts. When the Smith women learned the game, the only male allowed to watch was the college president, one of supposed sufficient dignity and age as to avoid unwholesome thoughts while watching graceful female athletes.

A Smith College star, Maude Sherman, married Naismith. But she and her teammates had not played by her husband's rules. Believing that women were "unaccustomed to exercise, and for the most part adverse to it," the organizers tried to protect players by having nine women on each team and requiring that three stay in one of three sections into which the playing floor was divided.[14] A two-section, six-player women's game would not appear until 1938. By 1896, California women drew hundreds of female fans to games, including a match in which Stanford defeated Berkeley 2–1 (each basket counted one point).

During the 1890s, the YMCA took over the game and spread basketball up and down both coasts. As early as 1892, Brooklyn contracted basketball fever. In Philadelphia it threatened to take over all the city's gymnasiums. Audiences turned violent, especially when referees made unpopular rulings. As historian Keith Myerscough phrased it, YMCA officials began to recoil from Naismith's "Frankenstein-type monster that was now creating havoc in certain quarters." The Frankenstein only grew larger.[15]

And entrepreneurial. In 1896, a group of Trenton, New Jersey, players discovered they could make money from charging admission. Each player received fifteen dollars per game, a princely sum during the economic depression of the mid-1890s. When they defeated a Brooklyn team

16-1, "The Trentons" began an American tradition by entitling themselves "World Champions." Within two years, an entire professional league appeared—six teams in New Jersey and Pennsylvania—which lasted until 1903. Basketball, it seemed, could produce profits as well as save souls. This was too much for Naismith's old YMCA boss, Luther Gulick. "When men commence to make money out of sport, it degenerates," Gulick lamented. "It has resulted in men of lower character going into the game." The YMCA would not allow "The Trentons" to play in a Y gymnasium.[16]

It no longer made much difference, however, what the YMCA did. Basketball was not only profiting play-for-pay teams, but producers of equipment. Albert Spalding, for example, had grown wealthy by the 1890s making baseball gloves, balls, and bats. He planned to be the John D. Rockefeller of sports: as Rockefeller ruthlessly integrated the global oil business from drilling to sales, Spalding integrated the sporting-goods business from his own manufacturing plants to sales in over twenty thousand retail accounts. Spalding even went Rockefeller one better: he published and distributed tens of thousands of guidebooks that instructed players and audiences about rules, while providing information about teams. Not surprisingly, the rules often called for Spalding equipment. As Naismith's soccer-type ball gave way to an inflated basketball (slightly larger than the modern version), Spalding efficiently produced and sold the new ball, now standard for the game.[17]

Basketball was also becoming international. Two years after the 1891 game at Springfield College, a YMCA instructor introduced the sport in France. It had already been played by British women that year and by British men the year before. In 1894, YMCA missionaries supervised the first contests in China and India, and Persia soon joined the list. Canada produced both the sport's founder and many players on the early Springfield College teams.

The game, however, would not become an international phenomenon until Michael Jordan appeared on the scene. In its early years, it was largely American, with some popularity in Canada and Western Europe. More precisely, it was an American city game. The first dribbling of the ball (instead of merely passing), apparently occurred on a Philadelphia playground in the late 1890s. The wave of immigrants entering the United States between 1890 and 1914 discovered the sport in city settlement houses, YMCAs, and even places of worship. It seemed nearly perfect for new arrivals. The game could be played on small city lots; the players needed nothing more than a ball and some kind of hoop. Jewish youngsters came to dominate New York City tournaments. After all, as *The American Hebrew* observed, the sport required "quick thinking, lightning-like rapidity of movement and endurance; it does not call for brutality and brute strength." And for the immigrants, it was unquestionably an American game. As Ted Vincent neatly summarized, "Basketball was the game of Franklin Roosevelt's New Deal urban coalition [in the 1930s] of Jews, Catholics, and Blacks."[18]

The first professional team to make a lasting mark on the sport was the New York Celtics (called the Original Celtics), formed in 1921. The Celtics, along with two teams made up of African-Americans—the Harlem Rens and the Harlem Globetrotters—became the most successful clubs in both profitability and in the way they reshaped the game, making it more fluid, graceful, and exciting to watch. These three teams dominated professional basketball during most of the first half of the twentieth century.

They were helped by new rules that changed the sport. Violence resulting from players chasing balls into the audience stopped when a high fence of chicken wire was placed around the floor. Players thus became known as "cagers," and fights with fans diminished. The wire was removed in most gyms by the time the Celtics and Rens appeared. But no rules could turn basketball into the non-contact sport Naismith wished for. One of the great Celtic players, Nat Holman, recalled that "We wore hip pads, knee guards, and an aluminum cup." Cut faces or "a loosened tooth were common injuries," he remembered. Players did not like to jump, one of them recalled, because "They'd just knock you into a wall."[19]

Yet with this crowd-pleasing bloodletting also came rules that encouraged crowd-pleasing imagination, speed, and subtlety. For years, baskets were simply attached to long poles. By World War I, however, they were on square "backboards" that allowed players to bank shots from fascinating angles. Until the 1930s, after each basket the referee stopped play and went to center court to toss the ball in the air for opposing players to tap into play. This break aimed at lowering the violence. By the eve of World War II, however, the center jump disappeared. Instead, the team that scored gave the ball over to the other team. Players, especially from the West Coast, began shooting daringly and quickly with one hand instead of launching the usual carefully planned, time-consuming, two-handed set shot.

By the late 1930s these changes helped make basketball the rage. *Time* magazine in 1940 believed that its seventy thousand teams made basketball America's largest sport. Women's basketball also grew popular again after some puritanical types, including First Lady Lou Henry Hoover, led a crusade in the 1920s to make the sport more "lady-like" and less exciting. The Amateur Athletic Union, which sponsored many women's sports, responded by running beauty contests at the women's national championships. The players themselves competed in the contests. Many angrily protested this kind of ticket-selling, as they did when professional teams, such as the Golden Cyclones—led by one of the greatest all-around athletes of the century, Mildred "Babe" Didrikson—played in shorts and jerseys. But, as historian Allen Guttmann noted, "The uniforms boosted attendance from under 200 to some 5000 a night."[20]

Unfortunately for the men, such uniforms did little to increase attendance at their professional games. The American Basketball League, with teams in middle-sized Eastern and Midwestern cities, lasted from 1926 until the Depression year of 1931. Those few in media who followed the pros preferred the stars playing with the Rens, Globetrotters, and Celtics.

Finally, in the flush postwar year of 1946, modern professional basketball was born, after a long hard labor. The ten-year-old National Basketball League (NBL) was challenged by a new league, the Basketball Association of America (BAA). The BAA had three strengths: its teams were sponsored by arena owners who had money as well as attractive places in which to play; these owners lived in large city markets where media attention and attendance were at a maximum; and the owners used their cash to lure away NBL stars—including one later selected as the greatest player of the 1900 to 1950 years, George Mikan. At 6´10″, Mikan was the first well-coordinated giant who could both dominate a game and pull in fans who would pay to watch his graceful hookshot. By 1949, the NBL surrendered. The two leagues merged into the National Basketball Association (NBA) that has embodied the professional sport throughout the rest of the century.

In the 1950s it was clear that smaller cities such as

Syracuse and Rochester, New York, could produce good teams, but not enough fans and media to pay for stars. Thus the 6´10˝ All-American of the University of San Francisco, Bill Russell, announced he would not play in a small city such as Rochester, which had draft rights to him. The Boston Celtics worked out an intricate deal to obtain Russell. He led Boston to eleven championships in thirteen years. By 1963, the Rochester and Syracuse franchises had moved to larger metropolitan areas. The NBA thus was located in, and ultimately saved by, the biggest media markets.

In 1952, the Dumont Television Network first aired a pro game. Two years later, the NBA dramatically sped up the game by introducing the twenty-four-second clock. Now the team having the ball could no longer slow the pace or stall while ahead; it had to shoot within twenty-four seconds. The speedy game, with its restricted space that a camera could easily cover (as opposed, say, to base-ball, where television could at any moment show only a part of the action), already lent itself well to television. The NBA Commissioner, businessman Maurice Podoloff, saw to it that teams supplied free player photos to the media. He strongly discouraged team owners from releas-ing bad news (such as low gate receipts). Podoloff and the NBA were beginning to understand the importance of marketing and public relations, and how to manipulate both.

In the 1960s and early 1970s, the NBA reached new heights of popularity and profit. Fans avidly followed indi-vidual matchups, especially the intense rivalry between two African-Americans, Boston's Bill Russell and Philadelphia's 7´1˝ Wilt Chamberlain who, except when guarded by Russell, was the game's greatest scorer. In 1975 a rival league tried to tap into the game's popularity. The American Basketball Association, however, lacked the financial backing, big-city media markets, and television contracts now required for survival. By the time Michael Jordan turned professional, the ABA had been forced to merge with the NBA.

But as Jordan left Chapel Hill, the NBA itself was stumbling. Revelations of extensive drug use by players, increased violence on the court, and the retirement of Russell and Chamberlain began to raise the question of whether professional basketball could survive. The ABA, however, had given the NBA a life-saving present: Julius "Dr. J" Erving, whose leaping, floating, and slam dunks astonished fans. Erving's elegance, both on and off the court, helped cleanse the game and prepared the sports world for Michael Jordan. And back of Erving stood the ghosts of at least a half-century of great African-American players who had overcome immense obstacles to prepare the world for Erving, Jordan, and others.

## *The Legacy of the Harlem Rens and "Dr. J."*

The most popular and profitable American sports have usually cut across class, ethnic, and ultimately racial lines. Basketball was devised in a small city college, spread rapidly to the great urban areas where new immigrants huddled together, and became the game of choice in rural Kansas and Indiana, where bent hoops on the sides of barns or garages served as goals. The game, especially the professional game, developed its ever-changing orginality and greatest popularity, however, in the dirt (or, if especially fortunate, the asphalt playgrounds) of cities. Historian Steven Riess estimated that through the late 1980s, almost 90 percent of all professional basketball players came out of urban areas. Nearly one-third emerged from New York City alone.[21]

Three-quarters of the leading players Riess studied

were German, Jewish, or Irish. Thus basketball could become a fast track out of immigrant neighborhoods, Hell's Kitchen, and lower-class row houses. But that track also included college. Nearly 75 percent of professional players attended an institution of higher learning. A full 95 percent of the players examined later worked in white-collar jobs, such as law and business executive positions. Their education, not basketball, made them comfortable and sometimes wealthy. But basketball did help realize one version of the so-called American Dream.

When Michael Jordan joined the Chicago Bulls, half of the NBA's players hailed from the twenty largest cities, usually inner-city neighborhoods where African-American families had replaced the Jewish, German, and Irish. Blacks had played on many of the earliest YMCA teams during the 1891 to 1941 years, then set up their own athletic clubs, such as the Smart Set Club of Brooklyn. These clubs were racially segregated, like schools and just about every other public facility. Philadelphia was different. Its schools were integrated, its basketball highly competitive. In other places, however, segregation forced black teams to play in broken-down gyms with shoddy equipment.

None of which prevented African-Americans from playing top-level basketball. By 1909 their skills led to the formation of the first important black professional team, the Monticello Delaney Rifles of Pittsburgh. Its creator, Cumberland Posey, came from an upper-class African-American family and had an incisive business sense. His teams generated controversy (and gate receipts) by physically intimidating amateur opponents. He saw to it that the Rifles were well covered by black-owned newspapers. When his Loendi Big Five team played an all-Jewish club team, the press and paying fans turned out by the thousands.

Posey's success set the stage for the Harlem Renaissance (or Rens) from New York City, the Harlem Globetrotters (who were, in fact, out of Chicago), and other squads of African-American players. The Rens played amid the Harlem Renaissance—that period of innovations, especially in music, literature, and art, that did much to transform American culture during the 1920s. The name of the team actually came from the Harlem Renaissance Ballroom on 135th Street, where players shared the room with the great bands of Count Basie and Jimmie Lunceford. These players made as much as a thousand dollars a month, a significant amount when fine apartments rented for less than a hundred dollars per month. But they had to barnstorm most of the year, often play two or three games a day, and eat in segregated restaurants while searching out segregated restrooms. One player recalled the team "slept in jails because they wouldn't put us up in hotels . . .; we'd spray all the bedbugs before we went out to play and they'd be dead when we got back."

The Rens and the Original Celtics were perhaps the nation's two best basketball teams. But when the play-for-pay American Basketball League appeared in 1926, neither joined. The Rens were excluded because of racism. The Celtics were shackled because the ABL's whites-only rule prevented them from playing highly profitable games against the Rens. After the National Basketball League appeared in 1937, it too refused to invite either the Rens or the Globetrotters. When the Rens played their last game in 1949, they had won 2,318 games and lost only 381, even though many had ended in fights with white fans who could not stomach losing to African-Americans. John Wooden, the UCLA legend who as coach won more college championships than anyone else, recalled the Rens as "The greatest team I ever saw."[22]

The Globetrotters meanwhile set a new style with flashy dribbling and behind-the-back passing. Many whites, as historian Jim Naughton records, "looked down their noses at the Globies, and considered them nothing more than a minstrel show."—until the team took two of three games from the great George Mikan and his NBA champion Minneapolis Lakers in 1948. Under the leadership of their imaginative business manager, Abe Saperstein, the Trotters were both profitable and good. The media trumpeted that the 52,000 attending a 1968 college game in Houston was an all-time attendance record, but the Globetrotters played in outdoor stadiums before 75,000 in Berlin and 50,000 in Brazil. The Globetrotters could legitimately claim to be the best-known basketball team, perhaps the best-known sports team, on earth by the 1940s and 1950s.[23]

The historic turn came in 1946–1949. The new Basketball Association of America, fighting to keep up with its wealthier rival, the NBA, signed its first African-Americans to contracts. In baseball, Jackie Robinson and Larry Doby broke the color barrier. The NBA finally surrendered. Its New York, Boston, and Washington teams signed African-American stars in 1949–1950. When the Boston Celtics and New York Knicks lured away a couple of Globetrotters, it marked the beginning of troubled times for the famous team. This infusion of talent, combined with the new television contracts, made pro basketball quite successful in the 1950s and 1960s, at least in the large-city media areas.

In 1972 the way opened for women. Title IX of the 1972 Federal Education Act forbade "Sex-discriminatory programs . . . by all educational institutions that receive federal money." Furious opposition arose from some male athletic directors and alumni. They claimed that women's sports would never pay their own way. (In truth, even among men's college sports, only football and basketball usually paid their own way.) But women, after all, had been playing basketball since its founding, and they now demanded equal conditions and equipment. With the aid of lawsuits filed against foot-dragging colleges, the number of women's hoop teams leaped from 242 in 1974 to over 1,500 in 1980. In 1978, the Women's Basketball League was formed.[24]

Both female and male African-American athletes now could play for pay. But as Michael Jordan entered the NBA, racism continued to pervade the sport. Oscar Robertson, the game's first big guard (at 6´5″) had dominated every level of play. His teams had won the Indiana high school championship; at the University of Cincinnati he became the first college player to lead the nation in scoring three consecutive years; and then, with Kareem Abdul-Jabbar, Robertson led Milwaukee to the 1971 NBA championship. But despite these achievements, and a squeaky-clean public life, Robertson, as an African-American, was not offered a single product endorsement until he had been a professional four years—and that offer was only to endorse a basketball. An unwritten, but acknowledged, rule among advertisers had it that black players' endorsements did not sell products.[25]

When the upstart American Basketball Association failed and was partly absorbed into its NBA rival, word spread that its collapse was due to 75 percent of its players being African-American. After the Dallas club released four of its ten black players, a team official declared, "Whites in Dallas are simply not interested in paying to see an all-black team and the black population alone cannot support us."[26] By the mid-to-late 1980s, the three NBA stars who received the highest salaries were African-Americans: Earvin "Magic" Johnson ($2.5 million), Moses Malone ($2.1 million), and Kareem Abdul-

Jabbar ($2 million). But two statisticians who analyzed overall salaries concluded that "when we control for performance, league seniority, and market-related variables, blacks are paid less than whites [in the NBA] by about 20 percent, or about $80,000 per year." This amount "is similar in percentage terms to the pay gap between blacks and whites in the general labor force."[27]

By the 1970s and early 1980s, African-American players not only suffered discrimination in product endorsements and salary. They also suffered from the eruption of a national debate, a debate that heatedly argued the question of why they had become so dominant in college and professional basketball. By the 1980s, they accounted for about 80 percent of starting players on pro teams. On the other hand, it was widely noted that even as late as 1987–1988, only four black head coaches and two African-American general managers worked among the twenty-three NBA teams. In the 1960s, the whispered reason for such a difference was that African-Americans had the bodies for athletic skills, but not the brains for management.

The whispering became a blast in 1968 when Charles Maher published a series of articles on the question in the *Los Angeles Times.* Many of the people Maher interviewed agreed with John Wooden, who had won eleven national championships at UCLA with black stars. "I think [the African-American athlete] has just a little more ambition to excel in sports," Wooden declared, "because there aren't enough other avenues open to him." The explanation then, lay not in different bone structure, but in the different opportunities American society opened to whites as opposed to blacks. Three years later, Martin Kane came to different conclusions in a widely noted *Sports Illustrated* article. Kane concluded that racial differences, not socioeconomic opportunities, explained the dominance of the African-American athlete.[28]

Even during quiet times, such a debate would have sparked heated arguments. But this debate appeared during some of the country's most transforming and violent years since the Civil War. Race riots burned and killed in North and South between 1964 and the early 1970s. In this supercharged atmosphere, experts angrily attacked Kane. Harry Edwards, the noted African-American sociologist, condemned Kane's methodology and evidence, while arguing that more differences always existed within any racial group that between such groups. The idea that slavery had weeded out the physically weak and led to dominant athletes a century or more later was not only false on the evidence, Edwards charged, but allowed whites to reinforce the old stereotype that while they might be physically inferior, they were intellectually superior to blacks. A few leading African-American athletes, however, seemed to disagree with Edwards. A 1977 *Time* magazine story quoted such black stars as football player O. J. Simpson of the Buffalo Bills saying, "We are built a little differently—built for speed." Joe Morgan of baseball's Cincinnati Reds (and later a leading television sportscaster) agreed with Simpson.

The controversy and, too often, racism that swirled around the debate was only part of the NBA's problems by 1983. Stories of drug use among players became front-page news. In 1976, the player's union and NBA owners had agreed to a new collective bargaining arrangement that first led to a rapid escalation in salaries, then—as the owners tried to save money—to bitter labor disputes. Fans were growing tired, moreover, of the style of play, especially a lack of discipline and defense, as well as the violence. Thus television also lost interest in the NBA. The

1980 championship game showcased Magic Johnson of Los Angeles against Julius Erving of Philadelphia, but CBS television only ran the game on tape delay around midnight after the local news.

At least ten of the NBA teams were either for sale or faced bankruptcy. Only six enjoyed profits. "It's just difficult," one team official reasoned, "to get a lot of people to watch huge, intelligent, millionaire black people on television." *Newsweek* simply concluded that the NBA "has become the sorriest mess in sports."[29]

Then a new era began. The just-appointed commissioner of the NBA was a young lawyer, David Stern. He helped work out a 1983 agreement between players and management that capped salaries and thus gave the poorer teams (usually in the smallest television markets) a chance to compete for players and thus a chance to survive. Stern also initiated a tough drug policy. It helped first offenders receive assistance and get off drugs, but threw repeat offenders out of the league.

And in 1984 Jordan joined the Bulls, a losing, lackluster team that had done little for the NBA in one of the nation's most glamorous television markets. His appearance climaxed a long process that began with James Naismith's imagination, the Harlem Rens' steely discipline and athleticism, Julius Erving's grace, and the post-1979 black-white competition that had erupted between the intensely joyous Magic Johnson of Los Angeles and the joyously intense Larry Bird of Boston. This long history now began, under David Stern's guidance, to move toward the limitless possibilities offered by the world's love of sports—and by a new global technology that U.S. transnational corporations and certain athletes could profit from mightily.

# CHAPTER II

# *The Globalization of Michael Jordan*

When Michael Jordan joined them in the autumn of 1984, the Chicago Bulls were on the ropes. They had won twenty-seven and lost fifty-five games the previous year. A typical crowd filled only one-third of the Chicago Coliseum's seats. The franchise's estimated worth was $18.7 million—only a fraction of some other franchises—and dropping. Television audiences were disappearing.[1]

Within the next ten years, Jordan became the most widely recognized and probably wealthiest athlete on earth. The Bulls sold out the old Coliseum, then their new United Center, and had thousands of names on a wait-list for season tickets. The franchise's worth exceeded $190 million and was climbing. The NBA meanwhile became a television goldmine not only in the United States, but globally. It was quite a decade—an era made possible by Jordan's athletic skills, his marketing instincts, a new type of corporation exemplified by Nike, and the technology of communication satellites and cable that made the globe into one mammoth television audience.

The outlook was not rosy in 1984–1985. Jordan had led the 1984 U.S. Olympic team to a gold medal in men's basketball. He charmed hundreds of millions of television viewers when he placed his gold medal around Deloris Jordan's neck. The publicity that trumpeted him into Chicago, however, did not endear him to his veteran teammates. Nor, more importantly perhaps, did his all-out intensity during practices, or his refusal to drink or take drugs afterwards. If some of the Bulls were losers on the court, they were self-styled champions off the court in Chicago's Rush Street and other late-night hangouts. Jordan seldom joined them.

"The first NBA game I ever saw was the one I played in," he later told reporter Bob Greene.[2] In that contest Jordan scored 16 points as the Bulls defeated Washington 109–63. During his first season, one writer later observed, "Jordan mesmerized crowds with his Nijinskyesque physical artistry and, especially, his balletic slam-dunks."[3] Experts were awed by his all-around game, including rebounding and, especially, defense. He shut down the other team's best guard or forward, while displaying uncanny talent for intercepting passes.[4]

Critics who searched for weakness soon thought they had discovered it: Jordan seemed not only unable to bring his teammates up to a championship level, but he often alienated them with his intensity, the parading of his skills, and his commercial successes off the court. These successes appeared at the start when, for $200,000, he endorsed a basketball for Wilson Sporting Goods. Wilson then terminated agreements with other stars, including Detroit's Isiah Thomas. At the 1985 All-Star game in Indianapolis, Jordan stood out as the only rookie elected to the Eastern Conference's starting team. When he appeared for a shooting contest, however, the rookie wore clanking gold chains and a sweatsuit loudly bearing the Nike logo. It proclaimed another highly profitable endorsement.

Thomas, Magic Johnson, Larry Bird, and others froze Jordan out of their company. In the game itself, the West All-Stars targeted and humiliated Jordan. His teammates looked the other way.[5]

The Bulls' young star proved to be a quick study. The gold chains disappeared. Humility and deference to his elders on the basketball floor replaced the swaggering. He went on that season to become only the third person in NBA history to lead a team in scoring, rebounding, and assists. Home attendance doubled. When the Bulls stumbled into the playoffs, however, Milwaukee quickly eliminated them.

The next season, 1985–1986, was pivotal. A wealthy Chicago real-estate developer, Jerry Reinsdorf, bought the team. Housecleaning began. Reinsdorf fired Rod Thorn (the general manager who had bemoaned having to draft Michael Jordan), and replaced him with a rumpled former sportswriter and scout, Jerry Krause. Known as "Gerbil," because of his shape, Krause hired a new coach, Stan Albeck, and demonstrated a unique gift for judging and obtaining talent. Jordan responded by intensifying his game. He won admirers when he cracked a bone in his left foot, missed sixty-four games, and then against medical orders returned in March to drive the Bulls into the playoffs. There the Bulls met Larry Bird and the Boston Celtics, who would go on to win the NBA championship. Jordan played two of the greatest games in NBA history, including the second when he set a playoff record of 63 points and forced a second overtime by hitting two foul shots with no time showing on the clock. Bird, who had scored 36 points, told reporters, "I think he's God disguised as Michael Jordan."[6]

During the 1986–1987 season, the Bulls' star won his first of seven consecutive scoring titles with a remarkable

37.1 per-game average. But despite a new, intense coach, Doug Collins, the team's forty wins and forty-two defeats sank them to fifth place in their Central Division.

Jordan, Bird, Johnson, Thomas, and other stars were meanwhile propelling the once down-and-nearly-out NBA to new heights of popularity. Basketball was challenging baseball and football as the national sports pastime. In 1986, much of the game's hope, charm, and popularity was captured in the film *Hoosiers,* starring Gene Hackman, Barbara Hershey, and Dennis Hopper. The film told the real-life David-and-Goliath story of tiny Milan defeating taller and deeper large-city teams to win the 1954 Indiana State High School Championship. Basketball was acquiring a kind of mythic quality. With grit and discipline honing talent, anything was possible.

Anything, that is, except a Chicago championship. Krause manipulated the draft so he could obtain Scottie Pippen, a forward from the University of Central Arkansas. The youngest of eleven children, Pippen, like Jordan, spent much of his childhood in the non-urban South. And like Jordan, he could shoot from any distance, pass, rebound, and play exquisite defense. Phil Jackson, then a Bulls assistant coach, believed that "Scottie had a near-genius basketball IQ."[7] Jackson also noticed that while other players seemed reluctant to get too close to Jordan, Pippen tried to learn all he could from the star. As the two became friends, over the next decade Pippen developed into arguably the second-most valuable player in the NBA.

During the 1987–1988 season, the Bulls won fifty of eighty-two games. Jordan became the first NBA player to win both the Most Valuable Player and Defensive Player of the Year awards. In April 1988, as the Bulls had nearly tripled their attendance since 1984, Reinsdorf and Krause quadrupled Jordan's annual salary to $3.25 million over a new eight-year contract. But again, despite the presence of Pippen, the Bulls quickly fell in the playoffs to Detroit in the second round. The first round, against Cleveland, however, became legendary. Jordan won the pivotal game with what became known as simply "The Shot." Behind one point with three seconds to play, he took a pass, and, as *Sports Illustrated* later described it, "spins to the top of the key [the foul circle] and hits a hanging, double-clutch, 18-foot jumper . . . at the buzzer" to stun 20,000 Cleveland fans.[8]

On July 7, 1989, Krause fired Doug Collins and promoted Phil Jackson to head coach. Thus began both an extraordinary friendship between Jackson and Jordan and one of sports' best coaching records. A substitute on the New York Knicks' championship team of 1973, Jackson was an unusual person and coach who read widely and meditated daily. He learned from both his meditating and the Knicks' successes that teams, not individuals, won championships. "The day I took over the Bulls," he wrote in his autobiography, "I would create an environment based on the principles of selflessness and compassion I'd learned as a Christian in my parents' home; sitting on a cushion practicing Zen; and studying the teachings of the Lakota Sioux" in his home state of North Dakota. Lakota warriors, Jackson emphasized, did not try to be stars, but helped others, regardless of the cost, so the group could succeed. Owner Jerry Reinsdorf once told Jackson that most people were motivated by either fear or greed. Jackson replied that he thought they were also "motivated by love."[9]

Translated, the new coach planned to install a new system in which all the Bulls, not just Jordan, would be fully involved in both offense and defense. Jackson's intricate system was beautiful to watch, but difficult and frustrating to learn. It did turn the 47–35 record of the year before into 55–27 in 1989–1990. Nevertheless, Chicago again suffered an embarrassing defeat in the spring 1990 playoffs at the hands of the championship Detroit team. Almost as bad, Jordan had grown to dislike Detroit's intimidating stars—Isiah Thomas, Bill Laimbeer, and Dennis Rodman—personally. He publicly attacked his teammates for not standing up to Detroit's brutal style of play.

Jordan was becoming obsessed with winning the championship in 1990–1991. The obsession did not stem from his need for money, but his need to be the best. Between his $3.25 million Bulls salary and his endorsements, the $17 million total probably made him the world's richest athlete. A U.S. advertising-industry analysis further revealed that he was tied with another African-American, television superstar Bill Cosby, as the best-known and best-liked celebrity in the country.[10] Increasing amounts of Jordan's celebrity and money came from selling Nike sneakers in the United States and, indeed, around the globe.

## Enter the Transnational Corporation

By the 1990s, teenagers shot and sometimes murdered each other to steal Nike's Air Jordan sneakers and other athletic clothing. The shoes, which cost well under fifty dollars to make in Southeast Asian factories paying some of the lowest manufacturing wages in the world, cost up to three times that in stores. Customers of all ages willingly paid the huge profit to Nike because of Jordan's name, the highly advertised technology that went into the shoe, and the almost supernatural aura that seemed to surround Nike's world-famous Swoosh symbol and motto, "Just Do It"—which, critics claimed, was exactly the advice gun-toting teenagers followed to obtain their Nikes.

After Jordan had become the world's most glamorous athlete in the mid-1990s, Nike was a $9 billion company with about half its sales overseas. It spent nearly $50 million in research and development and more than a half-billion dollars on advertising and marketing worldwide, a figure that dwarfed the spending of such competitors as Reebok, Fila, and Adidas. Nike churned out profits not only by dominating its markets. The Beaverton, Oregon, company exemplified something new and most significant in American history: a corporation that made nearly all its products abroad and sold half or more of those goods in foreign markets. In other words, although known as an American corporation, most of its laborers and its sales were abroad.[11]

Multinational corporations are not new. In the late nineteenth century, such U.S. firms were rising from the ashes of the Civil War to dominate markets. These included Standard Oil in petroleum products, Eastman Kodak in film, Singer in sewing machines, and McCormick in farm harvesters. But these companies differed from their late-twentieth-century descendants in at least five respects.

First, the 1890s firms largely employed Americans to produce their product; in the 1990s, the firms extensively employed foreign labor and made the overwhelming bulk of their goods abroad. By 1980, a stunning 80 percent of these U.S. corporations' revenues came from overseas production, and less than 20 percent arose from exporting American-made goods to foreign markets.

Second, while the late-nineteenth-century firms largely traded in natural resources (oil, iron) or industrial goods (steel, paint), the late-twentieth-century firms traded in designs, technical knowledge, management techniques, and organizational innovations. The key to success was not so much the goods, as it was knowledge: the quickly formulated and transferred engineering and marketing information, the control of advanced, rapidly changing technology (such as how to make computer software—or Air Jordans).

A third revolutionary characteristic of transnationals, such as Nike or Coca-Cola, was their increasing dependence on world markets—not solely U.S.—for profits. For the corporations that drove the U.S. economy, and on which nearly all Americans depended directly or indirectly for their economic survival, relied in turn on global markets. In 1996 for example, the Atlanta, Georgia-based Coca-Cola Company, that most American of all firms, stopped dividing its markets between "domestic" and "international." Instead, it organized sales along the lines of specific regions and, in this regard, "North America" was not substantially different from, say, "Southeast Asia." This new policy was logical: in 1996 four of every five bottles of Coke were sold outside the United States.

A fourth difference followed: as the Nike budget demonstrated, transnationals of the late twentieth century depended on massive advertising campaigns to make people want their products. The advertising too was revolutionary in that by the late 1980s it could be instantaneously seen on as many as thirty to five hundred television channels in many countries through the new technology of communication satellites and fiber-optic cable. Such advertising often sold not merely a product (as sneakers), but a lifestyle ("Just Do It") that in most instances was based on American culture. Standard Oil petroleum or McCormick harvesters were not uniquely American products; they challenged other cultures far less in the 1880s than did Nike athletic equipment and its accompanying advertising lifestyle advice, which vividly illustrated the freedom (even the ability to fly through the air with a basketball) that seemed to come with the equipment.

Finally, because the old multinationals were not only headquartered, but produced and/or sold much of their product, in the United States, they could usually be made accountable to the government in Washington. Even the richest of all Americans, John D. Rockefeller, learned this hard lesson when the government broke up his Standard Oil monopoly into a number of smaller companies in 1911. The new transnational, however, became so global by the 1980s that a single government had power over only a part of the firm's total operation. The size of many transnationals, moreover, dwarfed the size of many governments. Of the hundred largest economic units in the world of the 1980s, only half were nations. The other half were individual corporations. Thus, for example, when the makers of athletic equipment were found in the 1990s to be exploiting low-paid Southeast Asians who worked in horrible conditions, the U.S. government's power to remedy the problem was limited. The transnational was, as its name declared, transcending the boundaries of individual nations.[12]

## Enter the Swoosh

Nike exhibited all five of the new corporate characteristics in varying degrees. It also shared another trait with this new breed of company, for it, like many other modern transnationals, enjoyed its greatest growth—its take-off into immense profitability—in the 1970s to 1990s. These are the years that, in reality, began the twenty-first century, for they produced the forces that will shape at least the early part of that century. During these decades, such new global technologies as computers, communication satellites, and fiber optics transformed the globe's economy. It should be pointed out that this new era in world history began not with the collapse of the Soviet Union and the end of the Cold War in 1989–1991, but with the appearance of the post-industrial technology nearly a generation earlier. For this technology changed the lives of peoples around the world and, in so doing, brought down the Communist system, which could not adjust to this revolution.

Phil Knight certainly had no idea that his company might be involved in such a transformation when he founded Nike in the 1960s. Knight, a red-haired and quite mediocre distance runner at the University of Oregon in the late 1950s, was also highly observant of the efforts of the legendary Oregon coach, Bill Bowerman, to produce a lighter, better track shoe. Knight recalled how the gruff, outspoken coach once painstakingly measured exactly how many strides a runner took in running a mile, then calculated that if just one ounce could be shaved from the shoes' weight the runner would be freed of 550 pounds during the race.

Knight carried this memory with him when at Stanford Business School a professor instructed his students to write a paper about how they would create a new company. Knight wrote a detailed analysis arguing that profits could be generated by importing cheap but well-made running shoes from Japan. Athletic footwear had been around since the 1860s when the British began wearing lightweight canvas leisure shoes. By the 1920s, Converse had turned these into the most popular and profitable sneaker in the United States. From then until the 1960s, nearly all basketball players wore Converse shoes. In the 1950s, however, German-made Adidas and Puma sneakers began to challenge Converse by giving free shoes to top runners who, in turn, would promise to wear them in competition. Thus German companies gave birth to the athletic endorsement several decades before Michael Jordan made it globally famous.

Phil Knight believed he could change American styles by using the Japanese to defeat the Germans. In 1963, while working in a Portland, Oregon, accounting firm, he went on an around-the-world trip. Knight carefully set time aside to visit Kobe, Japan, where the Tiger running shoe was produced. When the skeptical Japanese asked which sports company he was with, Knight made up a name on the spot—Blue Ribbon Sports. He asked for some Tigers to take back to Oregon. The tough Bill Bowerman admitted, "These shoes aren't half bad."[13] Knight believed he had found his opportunity. He and Bowerman each invested five hundred dollars to purchase Tigers, then Knight traveled around to regional track meets and sold the shoes from his car. The first year Blue Ribbon Sports sold one thousand pairs and cleared about $364.

By 1969, Knight's sales had leaped to a million dollars. He now worried that the Japanese, whose own transnationals were rapidly spreading around the world, might drop him so they could sell Tiger shoes directly to American customers. The two men, however, were determined to find better shoes. One Sunday morning, with his wife at church, Bowerman poured melted rubber into the family's waffle iron. Waffle-soled, square-cleated athletic shoes, made of lightweight fabric, were the ultimate result. Knight decided to concentrate on the shoes he and Bowerman were developing. But he needed a name, a trademark, an easily recognized symbol. One of his young designers, Jeff Johnson, had a bad night's sleep during 1971 in which he dreamed of Nike, the Greek winged goddess who symbolized victory. Without any better idea, Knight decided to try Johnson's suggestion.

The next year, a Portland State University design student, Carolyn Davidson, sketched a fat, floating check-mark as a symbol for the running shoes. "I don't love it," Knight told her, "but maybe it'll grow on me." He bought the design from her for thirty-five dollars. Nike employees called it the "Swoosh." By the 1990s, when it was worn by Nike endorsers Michael Jordan, golfer Tiger Woods, and tennis champion Pete Sampras, among many others, the Swoosh had become the most recognizable commercial logo in global sports. Davidson later received Nike stock from Knight, and rightly so. Her design made it possible for people in faraway lands whose languages did not easily translate the word "Nike," to identify Nike products simply by the Swoosh. Only an image, not words, was needed to reap profits in other cultures.

Knight and Bowerman viewed themselves as rebels. They rebelled against traditional shoemakers, older marketing techniques, and conservative officials who tried to control such sports as the Olympics—"a bunch of rich old farts," Bowerman termed these officials, "aristocrats looking for a trip."[14] Knight and Bowerman admired the athlete, the person who actually competed. They especially venerated athletes who were nonconformists, in-your-face free-thinkers. It was, after all, the 1960s and early 1970s. Knight encouraged these traits at Nike, where employees enjoyed themselves greatly by either constantly talking sports or gathering in strategy sessions known as "Buttface meetings" where they yelled criticisms at each other and even at the boss, who happily encouraged such clashes. One amused observer decided that "Nike is like high school, only with money."[15]

Knight was convinced that "Sports, unlike entertainment, functions as a meritocracy."[16] Results on the playing fields, not an athlete's hairstyle or family background, counted. So he and Nike embraced the champions who were different (and thus, of course, could also be easily identified by viewers). His first endorser was a long-haired, free-spirited, middle-distance track champion from Bowerman's Oregon team, Steve Prefontaine. For five thousand dollars, "Pre" wore Nike shoes and shirts as he broke seven track records. Knight and Prefontaine then directly, and successfully, challenged sports promoters who made money from amateur athletes, but who refused to allow the athlete to make money at track meets. When the twenty-four-year-old "Pre" died in an automobile crash, Knight named a building at Nike headquarters after him, then installed a life-sized sculpture of the runner. Another of Nike's buildings at Beaverton was named McEnroe (after the tennis champion and Nike endorser who seemed to scream at and insult officials as often as he defeated opponents on global courts). Eventually, a third building would be named Jordan.

In the late 1970s, the American addiction for physical fitness, especially by jogging, helped drive Nike sales from $10 million to $270 million.[17] Half of all running shoes sold were Nikes. But Knight wanted more. He was determined to smash Adidas and Reebok, his main competitors. Thus Nike continued to need large chunks of cash for development and expansion. The funds came not from U.S. banks, but from Nissho Iwai. This Japanese trading firm had saved Knight in the early 1970s when a downturn in sales threatened his company. Nissho Iwai continued for the next quarter-century to be the banker for this U.S. transnational.[18]

To overwhelm Adidas and Reebok, Knight also thought he needed more imaginative advertising. He did not reach this conclusion easily. Indeed, he had considered advertising largely a waste of money, even a fraud. Any product's success, Knight preached, should depend on its quality (and the success of its users, such as Prefontaine), not on slick advertising gimmicks. But Adidas and

Reebok employed advertising, so in 1980 he visited a local ad agency. "I'm Phil Knight," he greeted Dan Wieden and David Kennedy, "and I hate advertising."[19] Wieden and Kennedy overlooked this unusual introduction to design superb advertisements. After all, they were known in Oregon as "long-haired, bearded flower children" themselves.[20]

In this case, however, appearing to be members of the counterculture did not necessarily mean being hip: nearly all of Wieden & Kennedy's ads for Nike went into traditional newspaper and other print media. Knight believed television advertisements to be too costly, given their return. In 1983, he switched Nike to the much larger Chiat/Day Agency, which designed Michael Jordan's first Air Jordan television commercials.

For a number of reasons, Nike promptly went into a nosedive. Reebok quadrupled sales revenues to become the number one shoe. In 1985–1986, Nike profits plummeted 80 percent. Part of the problem turned out to be the need for more focused advertising. The much larger problem was that Nike employed nearly all men, who designed shoes for men. Women, however, were now buying as many athletic shoes as were men. Reebok shrewdly designed apparel for this booming female market. In 1986, Knight returned to Wieden & Kennedy. He brought with him Nike's new breakthrough, a basketball shoe with an air pocket in the inner sole. Knight agreed to advertise the new footwear on television. Dan Wieden came up with a slogan: "Just Do It." Two young women on Wieden & Kennedy's staff devised an ad with no words, only the Swoosh logo and the blasting music of the Beatles' "Revolution." They had found how the transnational corporations could sell goods in vast overseas markets, even in the many lands where English was not spoken. Nike sales soared. They doubled between 1987 and 1989 to $1.7 billion.[21]

Michael Jordan wore the new shoe, but, as Knight recalled, "it was so colorful that the NBA banned it—which was great! We . . . welcome the kind of publicity that pits us against the establishment." And Jordan, of course, "played like no one has ever played before. . . . Sales just took off." The Bulls' star was used to sell the new shoes, Knight emphasized, because "It saves us a lot of time. . . . You can't explain much in 60 seconds, but when you show Michael Jordan, you don't have to. People already know a lot about him. It's that simple."[22] Jordan, in other words, was an image much like the Swoosh.

David Falk had brought Knight and Jordan together in 1984. A 1975 law-school graduate, Falk and his ProServ agency were among the first professional agents who not only represented athletes in contract negotiations (in which ProServ took about 4 percent of the player's salary for negotiating the deal), but in obtaining endorsements (where ProServ could receive as much as 25 percent).[23] Falk knew what Oscar Robertson had learned the hard way: many companies did not want African-American athletes to represent them. In 1982, however, basketball great Kareem Abdul-Jabbar received an unprecedented fee, $100,000, for endorsing Adidas sneakers. Then Jordan's North Carolina teammate, James Worthy, received $1.2 million over eight years to wear a New Balance shoe.

Falk speculated that the right athlete could do more than merely wear a particular sneaker: that athlete could actively enter the marketplace, drive sales upward, then profit handsomely from those sales. He believed Jordan could be such a pioneer. The North Carolinian was not only a special player, but a respected person with good values instilled by strong parents. "The thing about Jordan," a competitor of Nike later observed, "is that he doesn't alienate anybody."[24] The All-American, moreover, was willing to work cheaply. At his first meeting with Knight, Jordan announced that in return for his endorsement he wanted, most of all, an automobile. Falk had had considerably more expensive terms in mind.[25]

The timing was perfect. Not only was Knight searching, and Jordan newly available, but the NBA had just appointed an ambitious, imaginative new commissioner. David Stern fervently believed that professional basketball could be promoted globally and be highly profitable. He later compared the NBA with Disney: "They have theme parks, and we have theme parks. Only we call them arenas. They have characters: Mickey and Goofy. Our characters are named Magic and Michael. Disney sells apparel; we sell apparel. They make home videos; we make home videos."[26] As one observer later noted, Stern "grasped the root law of capitalism: grow or die." The new commissioner, as Jeff Coplon wrote, had nothing less than a "manifest destiny regime."[27]

A key to making that destiny manifest, critics claimed, lay in the NBA achieving what historian John Hoberman called "virtual integration": white executive business control combining with African-American athletic domination to create a "crossover appeal" among millions of white and black viewers. Once the idea that the NBA was (in the words of one of its African-American executives) "too black," and "too drug infested," was "turned around," then the "new personalities" of Johnson, Bird, and Jordan could become moneymaking machines.[28]

Nike and Wieden & Kennedy found another African-American who had crossover appeal. The movie director Spike Lee scored a major success with all audiences in 1986 with his film *She's Gotta Have It*. The lead male character, Mars Blackmon (played by Lee himself), was such an obsessed fan of Michael Jordan that he even wore shoes endorsed by the Bulls' star to bed. Lee filmed advertisements (turned out by a young sports-addict-turned-writer, Jim Riswold) that brought "Mars" and Jordan together in some of the funniest and most popular commercials of the late 1980s. These combined with ads showing Jordan flying through the air for what seemed to be forever. "His Airness," as he became known, and the Air Jordan shoe became one. In 1987, Falk negotiated a seven-year contract with Nike. Phil Knight not only guaranteed Jordan $18 million, but a royalty on every Air Jordan shoe sold—a royalty that would amount to far more than $18 million.[29]

Nike was steamrolling its competitors out of the market. The first step had been to sign the most visible athletes, especially those known for having a sharp edge. Knight, for example, brought in outspoken basketball star Charles Barkley, who declared flatly in his television commercial that he had no intention of being a role model for youngsters. In other Nike ads, however, stood the ultimate role model for young and old alike, Michael Jordan. Another Nike role model was baseball-football star Bo Jackson. By 1991, a poll ranked Jordan and Jackson as the world's two most famous athletes—a ranking due largely to their global television commercials for Nike.

Knight then took another step to flummox his competitors. He signed not just individual stars, but entire colleges. These schools, famous for their sports teams, promised to use Nike equipment nearly exclusively in return for large sums of money. Football powerhouse University of Miami was first in 1989. As Nike's historian, Donald Katz, described it, Knight wanted "to vertically integrate all sports"—much as John D. Rockefeller's Standard Oil Company had vertically integrated the oil industry from exploration and drilling to selling gas at the pump. Knight was becoming the Rockefeller of the sports world.[30]

Nike's next step to crush competitors was especially significant. Knight launched massive global advertising campaigns. As he explained, "To paraphrase Willy Sutton [a criminal who said he robbed banks because that's where the money was], we're going out into the world because that's where the feet are." Nike had begun major advertising in Europe during 1985, then increased the pace until its shoes dominated that market. Jordan, now famous for both his Olympic basketball feats and his Nike ads, could no longer walk down many European streets by 1988 without drawing a crowd. In Japan, an all-out advertising campaign in 1989 made the Air Jordan shoe number one and, along with Coca-Cola, one of the two items teenagers said they most wanted.[31]

Nike also joined the many who had for decades, indeed centuries, lusted after the great China market. In 1978, the Communist government slowly began delicate reforms aimed at opening China to capital investments, while maintaining tough Communist Party political control. Nike became one of more than fifty thousand joint ventures between transnational corporations and the Chinese. By 1995, China was second only to the United States in receiving direct foreign investment. With annual growth rates of 8 percent and more (the average annual U.S. rate has historically been about 3 percent), the world's most populous market was booming.[32]

Many Chinese could now watch foreign television, notably shows from British-governed Hong Kong. When Nike opened its new store in the giant boomtown of Shanghai, hundreds lined up during the night to buy clothing. Knight put on a spectacular opening: "six scantily clad women—the few clothes they were wearing came from Nike's line—did aerobics," according to the staid *Far*

*Eastern Economic Review,* "to the tune 'New York, New York,' and Madonna's 'Material Girl,' fitting songs for the dawning of the age of the Chinese consumer."[33]

In 1991, Nike, with ads devised as usual by Wieden & Kennedy, launched the first coordinated around-the-world commercial to sell the new Air 180 shoe. The campaign cost $20 million. It began with Super Bowl game spots where some words of English were used. The ad was then repeated in more than a dozen European nations, but no spoken language was heard. The ads for the Air 180 featured Jordan, Bo Jackson, and Steve Prefontaine, among others. In blanketing major markets, Knight avoided only South Africa. That government's *apartheid* policy had so brutalized the majority black population that in 1986 the U.S. government began imposing economic sanctions on the white regime. Washington also pressured U.S. corporations to leave South Africa. Despite the brutality, and despite their own government's request, many U.S. transnationals were reluctant to give up such a profitable market. Nike finally left in 1989. Two years later, *apartheid* ended, a black government gained power, and in 1994, Nike reentered a market that could buy as many as twenty-five million pairs of shoes annually.[34]

## Enter the Communication Satellite

"Now the experience of sports is everywhere," Knight observed. "It's all-encompassing and instantaneous. It's right there beside you from cradle to grave" and is "the culture of the world." It was a remarkable claim: sports was the culture that linked the peoples around the globe. He could exhibit some persuasive evidence. Exhibit A was Michael Jordan. "I never knew it could be like this," the star remarked. He had been popular as a high school senior and especially in college, "but I never knew it could be nation-based—or, if you want, world-based."[35]

World-based also described the U.S. advertising agencies that created the images of the glories of American life. Of the fifteen largest agencies in the world, thirteen were American (the other two were Japanese). Nike's Wieden & Kennedy agency was not one of the largest, but it was certainly ranked among the most creative, known, and successful. Advertising took off globally as Michael Jordan soared in the 1980s. In 1980 the average American was exposed to sixteen hundred advertising messages each day. A decade later, it was about three thousand. Corporations were now spending so much on advertising and other promotions that it amounted to $120 annually for every person on earth.[36]

These agencies exploited such breathtaking technology as cable and communication satellites that, by the late 1970s, were bringing about not merely new communications, but a new age. Sports and ad agencies had long enjoyed highly profitable rides on the back of technology. As radio became a part of life in the 1930s, for example, baseball advertisers had used broadcasting to reach into many isolated corners of the country. Ronald Reagan, the U.S. President in the 1980s famous for being "The Great Communicator," learned how to communicate by broadcasting Chicago Cubs baseball games over a small Illinois station in the early 1930s. Reagan was not at the Cubs' ballpark; he read the plays off a telegraph wire and dreamed up much of the fill-in information he used to kill the time between plays. Baseball radio broadcasts were so popular and profitable that few minded if some of what they heard was untrue.

In 1936, regular television broadcasts began in Hitler's Germany. Berlin's Olympic Games were the first major televised sports event. Some 150,000 people could watch

the snowy pictures, but only in Berlin itself. U.S. televised sports started in 1939 with a college baseball game
between Columbia and Princeton. It was sent out to two
hundred television sets in the New York City area. The
next year, the first basketball game, a doubleheader college contest in New York City's Madison Square Garden,
was televised. By the late 1950s, the medium had grown
so rapidly and powerfully that professional basketball
franchises were being granted largely on the basis of the
largest media markets—that is, where the most profitable
television contracts could be negotiated.[37]

In the late 1970s and early 1980s, just as Jordan
appeared on the scene, commercial television began to
jump over national boundaries. A decade later, NBA
games, especially those of the Chicago Bulls, could be
seen in ninety-three countries. This exposure was made
possible by the direct broadcast satellite (DBS). The first
DBS was launched in May 1974 by the U.S. National
Aeronautic and Space Administration (NASA), which in
1969 had put the first men on the moon. DBS was to have
a much greater impact on the day-to-day lives of people
around the world than did the moon landing. Launched
into orbit so it would float in space over the west coast of
South America, the first broadcast satellite relayed information from specialists on health and education into pre-
viously isolated areas, such as parts of Alaska and the
Rocky Mountains. The experiment was so successful that
private companies stepped in to launch their own satellites. The companies, as usual, made their profits by selling advertising.[38]

Thus new technology led the world's people into a new
era of globalization, paid for by a new advertising. By the
1980s, the technology became even more dazzling—and
profitable. DBS went into the home of the television
viewer through one of two routes. One route sent the sig-

nal from, say, the stadium where the game was being played, to the satellite, then back to earth to individual receivers (or "dishes") owned by a viewer. In the 1980s and 1990s, however, the more common route was from the stadium to the satellite and then to a receiving station on earth where the signal went into cables. The cables carried the game into individual homes. Thus whoever controlled the cable service could go far in controlling the television markets.[39]

The potential profits of those markets skyrocketed in the 1980s when fiber-optic cables were developed. These new cables carried information in light waves along a silicon wire that had the thinness of a human hair. Compared with the copper wire it replaced, the silicon wire could transmit dozens of television programs at once, instead of one or two. The silicon, unlike the copper, was not affected by heat or moisture and could emit signals for a hundred years before wearing out. Digital compression technology meanwhile increased the possible number of channels on a television set from dozens to 150 and even 500. A British firm developed the first round-the-world fiber optic system in 1991.[40]

Now the possibilities were breathtaking. A single direct-broadcast satellite could transmit to earth all of the *Encyclopedia Britannica* in less than a minute. The contents could even be picked up and placed before the viewer by a cable relay station whose cost in 1975 had been $125,000, but in 1980 was less than $4,000 because of the quick technological advances.[41] Profits promised to have no limit. As cable and satellites created international television in the 1980s, so did advertising, whose profits for cable companies shot up more than ten times.

These new systems seemed to resemble magic cash registers as they churned out the money. They also resembled dynamite as they blew apart governmental regulations and geographical boundaries. They did nothing less than change some of the fundamental ways nations' officials behaved toward their citizens. Italy, for example, had allowed no private local television stations until 1976, but within ten years some three hundred private stations sprang up to cater in some instances to sports fans and, in most instances, to make money from advertising. Belgium had never allowed advertising on its stations. This rule changed, even on state-controlled programs, as the number of stations expanded.[42] Cable satellites and advertisers were also ready to exploit the newly-open markets of Eastern Europe after the fall of Communist governments in the late 1980s. The markets of Russia, after the Soviet Union collapsed in 1991, were also unshuttered. It was noteworthy when a nation, such as post-1979 revolutionary Iran's Islamic government, outlawed international advertising in the new era.

Whenever innovative technology appears, swashbuckling entrepreneurs quickly materialize to exploit it. In the 1880s and 1890s, it had been the robber barons (Rockefeller, steelmaker Andrew Carnegie, banker J. P. Morgan), whose understanding of industrial technology's potential made them very rich. In the 1980s and 1990s, those made very rich by satellite and cable included Michael Jordan and Phil Knight, but also such media barons as American Ted Turner and Australian Rupert Murdoch. For it was the few, led by Turner and Murdoch, who created the satellite-cable networks on which Jordan and Knight sold the NBA and Nike shoes to the many around the world.

Turner was a flamboyant figure—he was famous for racing yachts, going out with beautiful women (he finally married actress Jane Fonda in 1991), and, most important, visualizing the possibilities of cable. Starting with two small domestic cable channels, he created the twenty-four-hour CNN (Cable News Network) in Atlanta during

1980. Turner nearly went bankrupt in CNN's early months, but a decade later the network had 132 million viewers and enjoyed healthy profits. A turn came when he bought the Atlanta Braves baseball team and the Atlanta Hawks basketball club, then displayed them on his "superstation" to lure cable customers from around the country. The superstation utilized communication satellites to reach tens of millions of viewers. In 1985, Turner added CNN International, which, by 1993, was seen in 143 nations, including twenty-three in Asia and five in Africa. By linking CNN with China Central Television, he had the capacity to reach six hundred million more viewers.[43]

Turner banned the use of the word "foreign" from any of his stations' broadcasts. He understood that little was "foreign" anymore in the interconnected world of the late twentieth century, not even for the most isolated and parochial of Americans. *Time* magazine called Turner the "prince of the global village."[44] CNN became legendary not only because it carried news and advertising to billions of people, but also because it had developed the largest chain of foreign news bureaus of any U.S. network. These bureaus enabled CNN to be on the spot to instantaneously televise dramatic news events, such as the Gulf War of early 1991 and the Soviet Union's collapse later that year. In the White House "war room" stood rows of the most sophisticated consoles that brought information from U.S. intelligence sources around the world instantly. But atop those consoles were set televisions tuned to CNN to assure the highest U.S. officials that they were fully and immediately informed. Turner's CNN was pivotal during the post-1980 years in creating a truly global television that exhibited truly global personalities such as Michael Jordan. In 1996, Turner received

$7.5 billion for merging his business into Time-Warner Communications, thus creating an even larger and more powerful worldwide company.

Rupert Murdoch became Turner's greatest competitor. The two men came to hate each other. Because U.S. law placed severe restrictions on foreign ownership of U.S. media, Murdoch, born in Australia, became an American citizen so he could purchase leading U.S. newspapers, television stations (which he developed into the Fox Network), and magazines (such as the most popular of all, *TV Guide*). One competitor complained that Murdoch "basically wants to conquer the world, and he seems to be doing it."[45] By the 1990s, he controlled media, especially television, on six continents. He became one of the world's richest people because, like Turner, he saw the global possibilities of cable and direct broadcast satellites. His satellite-based Sky News linked up with European state-owned stations to form Euronews, which blanketed much of Europe. Murdoch also bought half of the Eurosport network that, after 1989, used satellite to reach twenty-two nations.[46] One of his most successful moves was to purchase Hong Kong-based Star Network and turn it into a system that enjoyed access to much of Asia, including the potential 1.5 billion Chinese customers.

Turner and Murdoch soon had to suffer some company in their quest for global markets. After all, as the entertainment journal *Variety* noted in 1990, "Sports have become one of European television's hottest commodities." The same could have been said for many other regions in the world. A giant transnational, Capital Cities, bought the ABC network in the United States, then used satellites to televise ABC shows, including sports, overseas. Capital Cities also created a satellite-based European Sports Network. Most notably, the company bought the highly successful, cable-based ESPN sports network in the United States. By the 1990s, ESPN was also seen in Latin America and Europe.

Because of cable and DBS, the far-seeing Turner, Murdoch, and Capital Cities covered the globe and generated billions of dollars in revenue. And because these giant media companies' international advertising featured the world's most recognized athlete, Michael Jordan, Nike (along with Jordan's other products—Wheaties, Hanes underwear, Coca-Cola, and then Gatorade) also churned out huge global profits. What could happen if Jordan and the Bulls won a championship, not to mention a string of them, boggled the mind. The championships were indeed won, but they were accompanied by tragedy. Again, of course, billions of people in the global village watched.

# CHAPTER III

## Bittersweet Championships

In 1989, *Time* magazine called Michael Jordan "the hottest player in America's hottest sport." Sportscasters were labeling him "Superman in Shorts." Although at 6´6˝ he was a full inch shorter than the average NBA player, Jordan, *Time* breathlessly proclaimed, moved in a world of his own, "a world without bounds. He gyrates, levitates, and often dominates. Certainly he fascinates. In arenas around the country, food and drink go unsold because fans refuse to leave their seats for fear of missing a spectacular Jordan move to tell their grandchildren about."[1]

This superman had no problem using his powers to create money magically. The Bulls sold out more games in eighteen months than they had during their entire history before Jordan arrived. Personally, he made many times his Bulls' salary by endorsing Chevrolet, McDonald's, Coca-Cola (then later Gatorade), Johnson Products (one of the largest and most profitable corporations run by African-Americans), and, of course, Nike. He became the first basketball player to appear on a Wheaties cereal box.

If, however, Jordan's skills translated into basketball records and wealth, they had not translated into a team championship. Americans, for all their immodest individualism, saved their highest praise for the Mikans, Russells, Johnsons, and Birds who raised teammates to a championship level. Many could score, but only a few could transcend individualism (that too often in sports, as elsewhere, was only a disguise for selfishness) to win it all. When legendary coach John Wooden was asked in 1990 to rank the greatest players, he chose Larry Bird and Magic Johnson, but not Jordan: "He's a show within himself, he's not a team player."[2]

Jordan's fans placed the fault on a lack of a good supporting cast. That might have been a problem in the mid-1980s, but by 1989, the Bulls had a talented team. Pippen was becoming the second-best all-around player in the league. It went, however, beyond the team. Chicagoans chafed when their hometown was called "The Second City." Given the history of the Cubs and the White Sox, Chicagoans never glimpsed even second place most baseball seasons. While Boston won sixteen NBA championships between 1947 and 1989, and even Minneapolis won five, Chicago's professional basketball teams had twice gone bankrupt and had reached exactly one conference championship (1972–1973—when they lost), in twenty-seven years.[3]

No one felt the failure more sharply than Jordan, simply because no one was as competitive. By 1989–1990, he was not only adjusting to Jackson's demands for a team offense, but making his own personal adjustments. For years this athlete who could not get dates in high school had been pursued by numerous women. It was not unknown for Bulls' practices to be interrupted by well-known actresses who were meeting him for dinner. Nor was it unknown for women to lie in front of his car and refuse to move until he talked with them. Jordan decided to eliminate such distractions.

In 1985, Jordan had met Juanita Vanoy, an independent-minded executive secretary for the American Bar Association. By 1987, they were making wedding plans, only to cancel them by mutual agreement. In November 1988, Jeffrey Michael was born. Ten months later, Michael and Juanita were married. On Christmas Eve morning of 1990, another son, Marcus James, arrived. The Jordans began planning a 26,000-square-foot house on eight acres in a Chicago suburb where the family could find refuge. Michael too seldom said no to the incessant demands on his time. Juanita, he knew, was more careful. "I have no problem saying no," she told *Ebony* magazine. "If someone doesn't step up and say no, there would be no time for his family. Everyone wants a piece of Michael. . . . I know it makes me look like a bitch," but "if that is what I have to be, then I will be a bitch."[4]

With his personal life in order, Jordan set out in the autumn of 1990 to prove John Wooden wrong. The season began badly. The Bulls lost their first three games. Then they won two in a row, including a rout of Larry Bird's Celtics. When the Bulls returned to Boston in February 1991, they were at full speed. Jordan scored 39 points, Pippen 33, as they whipped the Celtics by 30 points. "The Bulls are the best team I've ever seen," Bird announced. With a record 61 wins, 21 losses, and Jordan's fifth straight scoring title, the Bulls cruised into the playoffs, where they demolished the New York Knicks in three straight. They then defeated Philadelphia four games to one and, finally, humiliated their long-time intimidators, the former champion Detroit Pistons, in four straight games.[5]

Jordan and the Bulls then faced Magic Johnson and Los Angeles in the championship series. The Lakers won Game One. The second contest turned out to be pivotal.

The Bulls destroyed the Lakers 107–86, as Jordan sank fifteen of eighteen shots to score 33 points. During a 15–2 run that won the game, Jordan made a shot that became famous. He soared to the basket to dunk with his right hand, in midair encountered a Laker blocking his path, brought the ball back down, switched it to his left hand, then somehow glided to the left of the basket and banked the ball in to score—all before returning to the ground. Magic Johnson admitted that "he did the impossible, the unbelievable."[6]

The Bulls won the next three games and the championship. Even with a painfully bruised toe, for which he used a specially slit shoe to obtain some relief, Jordan dominated the games. He and the Bulls finally had their championship. He clutched the Most Valuable Player trophy after the final game, hid his head in Juanita's arms, and cried before tens of millions of viewers. He then apologized to reporters: "I never showed this kind of emotion before in public." The *Chicago Tribune*'s Sam Smith wrote that Jordan did not have to apologize: "He really is human" after all.[7]

## Selling a Championship

New York essayist and literary critic Stanley Crouch could say that Jordan played with "disciplined audacity."[8] Americans liked that kind of play because "the improvisational hero is the great American hero. Louis Armstrong, Fred Astaire, or Michael Jordan conceiving some sort of remarkable play while in motion." As if comparing a basketball player to an inventor of jazz (Armstrong) or a creator of modern dance (Astaire) were not sufficient, *Time* believed Jordan surpassed the *Mona Lisa:* "Modern life suffers from the Mona Lisa complex," the magazine gushed, "the idea that when you finally see a legendary work of art, it inevitably disappoints, appearing somehow smaller . . . than you had imagined it. Except Michael Jordan." Only the Bulls' star united "hard-court fundamentals with the improvisational creativity of the blacktop."[9] In other words, he played in the ordered commercialism of the twenty-thousand-seat auditorium, but with the imagination and seldom-seen skills exhibited on inner-city (or rural) playgrounds.

All in all, Paul Sullivan wrote in the *Chicago Tribune,* Jordan did not have "a bad year. He welcomed his second son into the world, had a hamburger named after him [McDonald's McJordan] . . . , agreed to let a network use his likeness in a Saturday morning cartoon, earned his second Most Valuable Player award, cut a commercial with [famed rock-and-roll musician] Little Richard . . . , hit a free throw with his eyes closed," and finally could wear "the championship ring."[10]

Sullivan's list was only part of the story. When *Sports Illustrated* gave Jordan its coveted "Sportsman of the Year" award for 1991, the article's subtitle read: "The consummate player and the ultimate showman, Michael Jordan has captivated America and is about to conquer the world." A leading sports advertising agent declared, "He has a level of popularity and value as a commercial spokesman that is almost beyond comprehension. It is a singular phenomenon. It never happened before and may not ever happen again."[11]

In 1992, Jordan earned about $25 million. Only $3.8 million came from his Bulls salary. The rest came from endorsements, including new deals with the Illinois State Lottery Commission, Guy Laroche (for making Time Jordan watches), and a restaurant bearing his name in Chicago. Not all the gloss turned to gold. Time Jordan attracted few customers. Other markets, however, seemed to be infinitely elastic. An unbelievable six million Wilson basketballs bearing Jordan's signature had been bought. Nike's Air Jordan remained the world's most profitable sports shoe.[12]

It was his success in the global market that set Jordan apart from the earlier commercial triumphs of Kareem Abdul-Jabbar and Magic Johnson. The NBA broadcast the Bulls-Lakers finals to more than seventy overseas countries. Nike featured six advertisements teaming Jordan and filmmaker Spike Lee, which had been widely acclaimed when initially shown several years later. The commercials worked well overseas. Rated the most "likable" and "familiar" of all performers in America, according to one poll, Jordan was becoming equally popular in some overseas countries.[13]

Soon after the Bulls won the championship, calls started coming in from Japan. "They want him for commercials," his agent explained. "I was just speaking to a broadcaster in Yugoslavia," a friend told Jordan, "and he told me you're the biggest star there. They see the games on tape delay."[14] Especially remarkable was Jordan's and the NBA's popularity in such countries as Italy, Spain, and Hungary, for they had long, successful basketball traditions of their own. Some of their leagues were considerably older than the NBA. But tradition seemed to be no match for communication satellites, global-minded advertising executives, the drive of David Stern's NBA marketing powerhouse, and Nike commercials.

Another dimension of Jordan's cross-cultural popularity in 1991 was revealed by a sports goods dealer in Skokie, Illinois, a Chicago suburb. "Michael Jordan is the same for everyone who walks in here. He is a hero," said Pradip Baywe, who had been born in India. "Anybody. Germans. Russians. Poles. Indians. Koreans. They are all looking for Michael Jordan, No. 23." The famous, sometimes infamous and bloody, ethnically divided communities in Chicago had found something in common. Meanwhile back in India, Pradip Baywe noted, his nephew wore Air Jordan shoes.[15]

This movement of commerce and culture went both ways. Europeans and Japanese flooded U.S. markets with their goods in the 1980s and 1990s. Gucci, Chanel, Benetton, Armani, and Italian-designed jewelery reached well over $2 billion annually in exports to the United States. And these upscale goods brought with them styles and smells that many Americans considered the standard for international elegance. But with the important exception of some Japanese and European automobiles and electronic goods, these products were styled and priced largely for the elite. American society showed increasingly wide gaps between the rich, the middle class, and the poor. The new post-industrial, information-technological revolution acted like earlier radical technological changes of the mid-nineteenth and late nineteenth centuries: they further widened the gaps between the classes and especially hurt the poor.[16]

Meanwhile, the NBA, Nike, McDonald's, Gatorade, Bugs Bunny, and other products associated with Jordan conquered the United States and spread across the mass cultures of Europe, Asia, and Latin America, made newly accessible by cable and satellites. European exports to the United States set some fashion standards, while American sports set new standards in reaching untold numbers of potential buyers. The $2 billion or so of the high-fashion exports into the United States were dwarfed by the many billions of revenue generated overseas by Nike, McDonald's, and Disney.

One major nation chose to fight this Americanization of its mass culture. France had long been proud of its own cultural accomplishments, not least its language—which, before World War II and the ascendancy of English, had been the language usually accepted as standard for conducting international relations. As early as the 1920s, many French complained that U.S. films, business techniques, architecture, and music were corrupting their culture. Americans noted, however, that most French did not complain. As writer Matthew Josephson observed while living in Paris, he found "a young France that . . . was passionately concerned with the civilization of the U.S.A., and stood in a fair way to be *Americanized.*" One of the great authors of the century, F. Scott Fitzgerald, followed out the logic while he lived in France in the 1920s: "Culture follows money," so Americans "will be the Romans in the next generation as the English are now." The French Ambassador to the United States seemed to show little delight when he had to admit to Americans, "Your movies and talkies have soaked the French mind in American life, methods, and manners. American gasoline and American ideas have circulated throughout France, bringing a new vision of power and a new tempo of life. . . . More and more we are following America."[17]

Some sixty years later, in 1982, a French Culture Minister dropped the politeness. Culture, as Fitzgerald noted, still followed capital. The French official warned of "American cultural imperialism." A cartoon appeared in 1986 showing the noble European continent defended by the great literary figures of d'Artagnan, Don Quixote, and Shakespeare against a U.S. attack—from the skies—led by Mickey Mouse, E.T., Marilyn Monroe, and a hamburger. The cartoon caught the problem rather accurately: culture was indeed becoming international, but it was not becoming harmonious. Europe's elite traditions were being blitzed from the skies (where the communication satellites roamed) by American mass culture. One critic put it bluntly: "The success of American popular culture abroad is due in part to the populist values on which it is based, [and is] more attractive to many of the common people . . . than the traditional values of their own countries."[18] The United States, moreover, possessed the capital and technology to ensure that the "common people" saw that culture.

Michael Jordan represented a movement not only threatening to overthrow the basketball dynasty of Magic Johnson and the Los Angeles Lakers. He and the products he endorsed also endangered traditional dress and even eating habits around the world.

## *"Basketball Is My Escape . . . Everything Else Is So Complicated"*

In 1991–1992, the Bulls set another record by winning sixty-seven of their eighty-two games as they conquered a second straight championship. After Jordan also won his second consecutive Most Valuable Player award, *Sports Illustrated*'s Jack McCallum wrote that he "stands alone on the mountain top, unquestionably the most famous athlete on the planet and one of its most famous citizens of any kind. . . . He *transcends* sports."[19] Jordan's dominance was tragically enhanced on November 7, 1991, when Magic Johnson announced that he had been infected with the HIV virus that causes AIDS, and that he would retire from the Lakers. Having become a close friend of Johnson's, the news devastated Jordan.

The 1991–1992 season was again a smashing commercial success for the Bulls' star. During the January 1992 Super Bowl, Nike ads gained international acclaim when they teamed him with Bugs Bunny on a basketball court. Critics ranked this "Hare Jordan" advertisement as the best of the day—a day that had become a kind of Super Bowl for hotly competitive U.S. advertising executives and their clients (who paid a million dollars for mere seconds of ad time during the game's time-outs). Phil Knight later said the Super Bowl ads had been "a big risk." "We invested in six months worth of drawings and a million dollars in production costs to show Michael Jordan, probably the most visible representative of Nike, paired with a cartoon character." But it worked: "We got thousands of positive responses."[20]

When *Newsweek* magazine listed the hundred most influential people in American culture, Jim Riswold was one of the select. Riswold was hardly a household name. But he was the writer who had turned out dozens of Nike advertisements since the late 1980s. Knight and Riswold so fine-tuned Nike's marketing that they had divided their global sales for basketball shoes into three segments. One was Air Jordan, by far the most popular. When that shoe lost sales, however, Nike produced "Force," which was represented by the burly Charles Barkley of the Phoenix Suns, and "Flight," represented by the balletic Scottie Pippen. "Instead of one big glop," Knight bragged, "We have the number one, the number two, and the number four brands of basketball shoes."[21] Adidas, Reebok, and the others had to take whatever Knight, Riswold, and Jordan left them.

In 1992, the United States put together the greatest-ever basketball team to represent the country at the Olympic games in Barcelona, Spain. The "Dream Team," as it was soon called, was led by Jordan, Pippen, Bird, Johnson (who came out of retirement for the games), and Barkley. As the Olympics approached, media attention grew so intense that the Dream Team chose to live in high-security seclusion apart from the other athletes.

Jordan was the focal point of the media and public. Each month, hundreds of babies in the world were being given the first two names of Michael Jordan. When Nike threw a mammoth press conference in Barcelona, a

Japanese correspondent asked, "Mr. Jordan, how does it feel to be God?"[22]

Julius Erving knew something about public adulation, but he was nevertheless stunned when he arrived in Spain. Jordan, "Dr. J" concluded, was less a person than "something of a 24-hour commodity." Erving and Jordan tried to get away from the crush by taking a helicopter out of Barcelona to a private golf course in the Pyrenees Mountains. By the time the two reached the fifth and sixth holes, however, the local inhabitants had spread word that Jordan was playing the course. People "started coming out of the bushes, down the hills," Erving marveled. By the time the two left there were "200 or 300 people waving goodbye to the helicopter. . . . I realized he needed some time to get away from the game and find some peace."[23]

Given Nike's genius in exploiting communication satellites and cable, it was not obvious where that peace could be found. At his last open public appearance, his biographer Jim Naughton records, Jordan went to a Dallas shopping mall where he signed autographs for an hour and a half, yet satisfied only a small number of the five thousand who overran both tight security and the mall. At a Memphis golf tournament for charity, huge crowds followed him in hundred-degree heat, while men tried to offer him hundred-dollar bills in return for an autograph.[24]

Several years earlier, Jordan had begun to try to retreat from such a crazy world. Once gregarious and spontaneous, he moved behind security, living in secret hotel suites. Sports columnist Mike Lupica later compared Jordan's determined attempt at finding privacy with similar attempts by the most legendary, and reclusive, baseball star of the post-1930s era, Joe DiMaggio. The New York Yankee great, however, had destroyed any chance to find seclusion by marrying Marilyn Monroe, who rightly considered the media and cameras to be her best friends. Not surprisingly, the marriage lasted less than a year. Jordan, on the other hand, had married in part to ensure his privacy. "Regardless of how available he is," Lupica wrote, "it's as if there is a line he has drawn between himself and the world. And he does not want that line crossed."[25]

Trying to draw such a line while being the center of global media attention during a long, nine-month season, or while he daily appeared in global living rooms through the power of Jim Riswold's advertising and the new technology that raced across boundaries—all this seemed to be a contradiction. As the new media developed after the early 1970s, as television moguls learned how to gain audiences and riches by exploiting this technology, they revealed the most private of experiences, then transmitted these revelations instantaneously around the globe. It sometimes seemed to be a symbiotic relationship. One partner maintained its celebrity and wealth by revealing deep secrets to the other, which, in turn, demanded more such secrets to maintain its audience. The media happily and lucratively kept the information and fascination flowing in both directions, while developing new devices to deepen the dependency. Given Jordan's fame and the squeaky-clean image he (and Nike, and his other endorsements), had so labored to create, it was only a matter of time before the media that helped make him would try to profit by breaking him.

As Jordan later admitted, he'd brought some of it on himself. In October 1991, President George Bush invited the Bulls to the White House for a celebration of their first championship. Jordan decided not to attend the ceremony. He said he had already met the President. Nor did he want to be the center of attention and take the limelight away from his teammates. The media speculated, however, that his absence might have more to do with Jordan being a registered Democrat who was not enthusiastic about the Republican President. Other media alleged that at the time of the White House ceremony, Jordan was playing golf at his retreat in Hilton Head, South Carolina, where bets on each hole supposedly reached four figures. When reporters caught up to ask why he had snubbed the President of the United States, Jordan uncharacteristically lost his control: "It's none of your business," he blurted out.[26]

Criticisms over missing the President's party had barely quieted before another barrage occurred. Jordan, his agent, and Nike threatened to sue the NBA for using the star's image without either their permission or their access to the profits generated by the wildly popular likeness of the Bulls' leader. The NBA backed down, but Jordan emerged looking to many like a greedy multimillionaire who willingly attacked the very system that had made him rich and famous.

Then, in late 1991, Sam Smith published *The Jordan Rules*. The star emerged from Smith's account as a selfish, mean, ghoulishly demanding egoist who physically beat, or launched tirades against, teammates when he thought they let him down. At one point, Smith charged, Jordan had punched teammate Will Perdue in the face when he decided the giant center had not played up to Jordan's standards. Of course no one, especially the earthbound Perdue, could approach Jordan's standards. Smith also claimed that he had been bitterly sarcastic in complaining about Bulls General Manager Jerry Krause. Jordan apparently made fun of both Krause's plump physique and some of his deals for players. As observers pointed out, however, in a half-dozen years, Krause had assembled a team that already owned two championships and had made Jordan not merely a scorer but a winner.

Coach Phil Jackson recalled that when the book appeared, "Michael was furious." Jordan had been careful to follow a discipline and a set of values that made him respected as well as popular. In 1984–1985, he had quickly taken off the gold chains and fur coat when he realized these might be misunderstood by the audiences he wanted to reach. Reporters noted that Jordan never allowed himself to be seen in public without fashionable, usually conservative, clothes. He did not even let himself be seen in the Bulls' dressing room without being fully and well dressed. He showered and dressed in the trainer's room, which was off-limits to the media, so he could always appear appropriately before the cameras. Jordan declared with conviction that if a person only saw him once for a fleeting moment in a hotel lobby, he wanted that person to remember him as proper, well-dressed, and respectable—which, indeed, he seemed to be.

That he had to endure growing criticism of his actions on and off the court was therefore most painful. He told *Sports Illustrated* that he always tried to be a "positive image" and a "positive influence." "I never thought a role model should be negative," Jordan declared. "If you want negativity, then you wouldn't have asked for Michael Jordan. You might've asked for [heavyweight boxing champion] Mike Tyson or somebody else."[27]

But trying to be a role model twenty-four hours a day in the televised fishbowl that seemed to be his life was, not surprisingly, difficult. As Erving had seen firsthand, there seemed to be no place to escape. "I look forward to playing now, more than ever," Jordan said in 1991, because it was the only place he could avoid the constant spying into his private life. "Basketball is my escape, my refuge," while "everything else is so . . . busy and complicated."[28]

Within another year, however, not even basketball

could be a refuge from alleged scandal and personal tragedy. Every allegation against Jordan, every sorrow he endured was, moreover, relayed to global audiences by cable and satellite. Nike was also coming under bitter attack. The gap between image and reality in the new media-made world of the 1990s was growing so wide that not even Michael Jordan could leap across it.

# CHAPTER IV

# New Frontiers—
# and Inner Cities

## Perils of Globalization

In mid-1992, Michael Jordan, his champion Chicago Bulls, and his U.S. Olympic "Dream Team" dominated the athletic world. His Nike ads had made the Swoosh a symbol recognized around the globe, while making Phil Knight and Jordan rich. In a year, however, both men came under savage attack. Knight stood accused of making Nike wealthy on the bent backs of exploited, poorly paid Asian workers. Both Knight and Jordan came under further fire for squeezing vast profits from, but otherwise apparently ignoring, African-American children who tried to survive in violent inner-city neighborhoods. Such accusations were only starting to build in intensity. By late 1993, Jordan stunned the sports (and advertising) world by suddenly retiring from the Bulls. An era seemed to have ended in the history of basketball and of sports marketing.

The accusations that Knight and Jordan ignored inner-city children had entered a new stage in 1990 when news stories spread of teenagers killing each other in Chicago, Houston, Baltimore, Atlanta, Detroit, and Philadelphia, among other places, simply for new sports clothing or sneakers. In Maryland, fifteen-year-old Michael Eugene Thomas was found strangled in a woods in May 1989. He wore no shoes. They had been taken by his killer, a seventeen-year-old who wanted the Air Jordans. In Houston, sixteen-year-old Johnny Bates was shot to death by seventeen-year-old Demetrick Walker, who then took Bates's Air Jordans. When the seventeen-year-old was sentenced to life in prison, the prosecutor pointedly announced, "It's bad when we create an image of luxury about athletic gear that it forces people to kill over it."[1]

Jordan, Knight, and Spike Lee (who had made the popular commercials glorifying the Air Jordan sneakers), quickly received some of the blame for the killings. Sports and editorial writers alleged that the three, through their advertisements, had made poor children so much want a status symbol the teenagers could not afford that they were willing to kill to obtain that status. Other young people sold illegal drugs to support their sports clothes habit. An owner of sportswear shops in Connecticut finally posted a sign telling customers to spend their drug-dealing profits somewhere else. The owner estimated he lost $2,000 in sales per week after he put up the sign.[2]

Spike Lee refused to take such blame. "The emphasis should not be on the sneakers or the Starter jackets," the filmmaker argued. "The emphasis should be on: what are the conditions among young black males that are making them put that much emphasis on material things?" Lee also blamed journalists for criticizing Jordan and him, but not blaming white stars, such as Larry Bird, who endorsed sneakers. Lee began to take some action. At a Nike All-American basketball camp in 1994, he told the young players they were "being used," and "the only reason you are here is because you can make . . . schools win and they can make a lot of money."[3]

Jordan remained quiet. He seemed confused. When reporter Bob Greene asked him what he thought should be done, Jordan replied that if a child was threatened, he or she should simply surrender the clothes. Greene asked whether parents should try to help by telling a child they would buy replacement clothes. Jordan thought that many parents could not afford another purchase. Instead, "They should say I'll [Michael Jordan] buy a replacement." A surprised Greene realized Jordan had not begun to think the problem through. The Bulls star told another writer, Rick Telander, that "I'd rather eliminate the product [the shoes] than know drug dealers are providing the funds that pay me."[4] He was sincere, but he did not stop his endorsements. In 1990, Nike alone spent $60 million on ads with the slogan "Just Do It." The company tried to atone to some degree by devoting $5 million to ads stressing the importance of an education and the necessity of staying in school.

The sneaker crimes soon became only part of a larger set of charges levelled against Jordan. He was perhaps the most widely admired African-American in a world where one of every four African-American men was in prison, on parole, or on probation. Nearly 40 percent of African-American men were found to be functionally illiterate. One of every three African-American children was growing up in poverty, even while living in the world's richest country. Jordan worked hard to be a role model, but the odds of a 20- to 29-year-old African-American playing in the NBA was 135,800 to 1 (and for Hispanics, 33,300,000 to 1.)[5]

Jordan stood accused of making a terrible situation worse: by spectacularly parading his basketball skills on the new media, he encouraged the young of all races to attempt the impossible and be like him. Critics claimed he instead should be sending youngsters a quite different message: that since they could never be like him, and since, contrary to what Nike said, they could never "Just Do It" in copying his athletic skills, they had to stay in school so they could survive in the new post-industrial era. Only such a symbol of that era, critics argued, could help convince youngsters, especially African-Americans, that sports was not going to be their ticket out of the inner city, while convincing others that these youngsters were interested in—and had talents for—things other than bouncing or dunking basketballs. In 1982, sociologist Harry Edwards had noted that "Blacks in sport . . . function in a semi-caste system relegated as they are to the least powerful, least secure, most expendable and most exploited population in the sports institution—that of the athlete."[6] Emphasizing that message, however, might sell fewer Air Jordans.

In 1990, these social and economic problems had turned political as well. In Jordan's home state of North Carolina, the popular former mayor of Charlotte, Harvey Gantt, an African-American, ran against archconservative U.S. Senator Jesse Helms. Gantt faced a steep uphill race. During his eighteen years in the Senate, Helms, who played to voters' worst instincts with his race-baiting and anti-civil rights record, had built up an overflowing campaign treasury, due in part to lavish gifts from the state's powerful tobacco industry. Jordan could have made a major difference in a race that went down to the wire. He was enormously popular in North Carolina, not least because of the true story that he continued to wear his powder-blue University of North Carolina basketball pants underneath his Bulls' uniform, partly for good luck, partly out of affection for his alma mater.

A number of African-American leaders, including tennis champion Arthur Ashe, asked Jordan to support Gantt publicly. Deloris Jordan did contribute, but her son never responded to repeated pleas. Close observers and friends blamed his silence on his commercial endorsements. As Julius Erving phrased it, "He has to consider the downside," and it is a "pretty heavy downside" if you "alienate half . . . or one-third" of your public.[7] Ashe believed that "advertisers want somebody who's politically neutered."[8] As a widely respected, even beloved athlete, who was outspoken in his demands for racial equality, Ashe had difficulty understanding those who were "politically neutered." Erving's point about the "downside" was no doubt true. In 1988, Jordan had signed a new, highly profitable deal with Nike, and by the early 1990s he and his agent, David Falk, had negotiated endorsement or licensing deals with at least fifteen businesses—deals worth millions of dollars. Gantt finally lost to Helms by a thin margin.

The new information-age marketplace could make you rich. It could also make claims on your soul. Jesse Jackson, the nation's most visible African-American political organizer, pointed out this danger in 1990. His organization, PUSH (based in Chicago), charged that although one-third of Nike's sales were from black customers, the company had few African-Americans in its management or on its board of trustees. Jackson also claimed that Nike refused to deposit profits in black-owned banks. He repeated the charge that Nike ads could lead to the poor dealing drugs and resorting to violence so they could acquire Air Jordans. When neither Nike nor Jordan responded, Jackson organized a boycott of Nike products.

Jackson hit a stone, or at least canvas, wall. The Swoosh proved stronger than PUSH. A poll showed that of those asked, about 39 percent agreed with Jackson's argument that a firm selling to African-Americans had a responsibility to return profits to those neighborhoods. But nearly two-thirds said that, regardless, they would continue to buy Nike products.[9] Again, Jordan remained silent throughout the controversy. Phil Knight and Nike did respond by sponsoring Spike Lee's antiracist television spots, putting money into youth groups, and—in an especially successful move—sponsoring many of the "midnight basketball" leagues that brought inner-city youths off the streets at night and into supervised neighborhood gymnasiums.

Jordan's friends believed his silence was not due entirely to his and his agent's neverending quest for ever-expanding markets. They argued that he had never had to face the kinds of discrimination and struggles earlier generations of African-Americans (such as Arthur Ashe) confronted. His parents had consciously played down race as a reason for anger. Their children were simply expected to excel, without excuses. They lived not in an inner city, but in a woodsy area three miles from an ocean beach. Laney High School was desegregated when Jordan entered. A friend recalled that "Laney seemed like a family back then. It had about a 6–4 white-to-black ratio, but it was really cool. No tension or anything." When he did face discrimination (as when a neighbor refused to let him use a swimming pool, or when a racial fight erupted at a University of North Carolina party), Jordan quietly exited. "Don't worry about race unless somebody slaps you in the face," he told a buddy.[10]

Some, especially advertisers and their customers, tended to see all this as evidence that Jordan simply transcended race. He was one of those rare public figures who appealed to all groups. Jordan certainly seemed to pull off this miracle in Chicago, one of the most racially and ethnically divided cities in the northern United States. He had also, however, demonstrated some sensitivity to the needy, especially African-Americans, but others as well. He had worked for the United Negro College Fund, for the Special Olympics, which supports athletic events for the disabled, and, later, he became involved in Ronald McDonald House Charities. He secretly developed an extraordinary relationship with a young Bulls fan who was dying from an incurable disease and worked hard for the Starlight Foundation, which helps children who are terminally ill. But his mother believed he could do more. In 1989, Deloris helped her son establish the Michael Jordan Foundation that contributed to African-American charities as well as the Ronald McDonald and Starlight Foundations. She tapped corporations and personal friends to raise hundreds of thousands of dollars each year to go along with Michael's own expansive giving.[11]

The problem, critics claimed, stemmed not from any selfishness or insensitivity on Jordan's part. Rather, when commerce clashed with social need, commerce too often won. Precisely because Jordan displayed such a sterling, appealing character, he was being pulled in all directions. By 1992, however, even his character came under fire. For the Bulls' star, this was the most agonizing charge of all.

## Gambling—and the Media

The story began in March 1992 with, as David Jackson of the *Chicago Tribune* nicely phrased it, "the type of men Michael Jordan's mother might have told him to stay away from." James "Slim" Bouler was a charming drug dealer who loved to jet to headline sports events and hang around headline athletes. In 1991–1992, authorities had seized $200,000 from Bouler, terming it money from drug (especially cocaine) and gambling profits. Among the funds was a $57,000 check from Michael Jordan.

Bouler first claimed Jordan had loaned him the money to buy a golf driving range. Police, however, concluded it represented Jordan's losses during high-stakes poker and golf matches at the star's retreat in Hilton Head, South Carolina. Jordan was well-known in Hilton Head for suddenly flying in on a private jet from Chicago for all-night poker. He was also known for laying a thousand-dollar bet on a golf putt. In South Carolina such gambling was illegal, a misdemeanor offense.

Then Jordan's name was linked to Eddie Dow, a bail bondsman. Also involved in shadowy nightclub businesses, Dow carried a loaded pistol and stainless steel briefcase full of cash to work each day. In February 1992, four men killed Dow, then took $20,000 in cash from the briefcase. Left in the briefcase were three checks totaling $108,000 from Michael Jordan. The checks were repayment to Dow for money Jordan lost during a three-day poker and golf excursion at Hilton Head in October 1991. The two also had often bet a thousand dollars per hole in their golf matches.[12]

When the news of the checks broke in 1992, Jordan was not accused of any crime. He was accused by sports writers of showing questionable judgment by enjoying the company of thieves and drug dealers while betting enormous amounts of money. It was precisely the kind of association that could make a person indebted to underworld characters who, in turn, could use this leverage to fix basketball games. No one accused Jordan of ever betting on basketball or falling under the control of such blackmailers. As he emphasized, moreover, betting a thousand dollars was for him equivalent to the average wage-earner putting a dollar on the state lottery. His bets hardly threatened him with bankruptcy.

Jordan nevertheless publicly admitted he had made a "mistake" in associating with such characters. He then added he had "a right to associate with whoever I choose," and that "There's nothing wrong with friendly wagers between friends."[13] The revelations did not hurt his basketball skills. During the height of the controversy, he scored 51 points as the Bulls defeated Washington. Nor did the news apparently lessen his market value: in the fourth year of an eight-year $25.75 million contract with the Bulls, Jordan announced he would not demand a new contract, but that he certainly deserved a much higher salary.

Friends defended him by arguing that such bets in cards or golf were simply an outlet for his uncommon competitive fire. He lived to compete. Always in motion, Jordan could not simply sit and watch television, unless he was criticizing films of his own basketball performances. The Bulls had even switched to a private jet for away games after Jordan and his teammates upset airline passengers by flinging loud taunts and hundred-dollar bills at each other in card games on commercial airliners. Such games were not uncommon among professional athletes. They were apparently addictive for Jordan.

As the charges erupted, Nike and other companies associated with him were notable for their silence. The air cleared, finally, in late March 1992 when the NBA investigated Jordan's betting and declared him innocent of any wrongdoing. South Carolina did not press charges because, authorities declared, the betting had occurred a year earlier and no one had come forward to press charges against Jordan. One South Carolina police spokesman was not as kind. "Absolutely, he [Jordan] appears to have been in violation of the law," declared a member of the Beaufort, South Carolina, Sheriff's Department. "But this is an incident that occurred last year, and no one has come forward, an eyewitness. . . . We've made some notes. My advice to Mr. Jordan would be start honoring the laws of Beaufort County. This is South Carolina, not little Las Vegas."[14]

The Bulls' star publicly apologized again. He also

backed down from his earlier defiance that he could associate with anyone he pleased: "I . . . spoke without thinking." "Sometimes," he noted, "you tend to forget as a
public person the things you have to take into account. . . .
The letting down of people is something I don't want to
encounter again." Jordan lamented that the media made
him appear to be "a 38-, 39-year-old mature person who
has experienced life to the fullest," while in reality he was
a "29-year-old who never really got the chance to . . . do
some of the crazy things" people in their twenties do. Such
justifications were weak, but he was closer to the truth, no
doubt, when he explained why he was (to use Arthur
Ashe's phrase), "politically neutered": "I don't think I've
experienced enough to voice so many opinions . . . , I
think people want my opinion only because of the role-
model image that has been bestowed on me. But that
doesn't mean I've experienced all those things."[15]

## *Wrapping Himself in the Flag: The 1992 Olympics*

With those words, Jordan survived the most dangerous
threat to his careers in basketball and global television.
Nike made no grand gesture to support him during this
time of trouble, but neither did Phil Knight attempt to
lower Jordan's visibility. The Bulls' star probably felt that
he owed some thanks to Nike for not ditching his
endorsements. In mid-1992, before the largest international media audience in history, Jordan vividly demonstrated that thanks—and immediately became swamped
in another controversy.

Jordan, Scottie Pippen, Charles Barkley, Chris Mullin,
David Robinson, and John Stockton were, along with
Larry Bird and Magic Johnson, leaders of the U.S.
Olympic basketball "Dream Team." The squad's appear-
ance on the gold-medal stand at the end of the games was

simply assumed, not least by opposing teams that were easily steamrolled. But the "Dream Team" was supposed to appear on the winner's stand in red-white-and-blue U.S. warmup suits that had a Reebok logo. Reebok had paid $4 million to the U.S. Olympic Committee for that valuable advertising. (The $4 million was part of $160 million paid by forty corporate sponsors to fund all the teams' expenses and training—and to have the sponsors' logos regularly in front of the worldwide audience viewing the games.)

Reebok was Phil Knight's most hated competitor. It was a company that differed from Nike not only because its shoes were different, but because its laid-back, cool company culture was the opposite of all the values loved by the freewheeling, hard-charging Knight. Jordan and Barkley, along with several athletes from other U.S. teams, announced they would not wear the Reebok logo. "I don't believe in endorsing my competition," Jordan declared. "I feel very strongly about loyalty to my own company." Notably, Pippen, Mullin, Robinson, and Stockton did not object to wearing the Reebok symbol.[16]

A media explosion erupted around Jordan and Barkley. They "think they're here representing Nike instead of the United States," columnist Dave Anderson wrote in the *New York Times.* Jordan is not "an alien from the planet Nike on loan to the Olympic team," Anderson added. "As for loyalty to his company, how loyal was Jordan to Coca-Cola when Gatorade offered him more money" and he quickly dropped Coca-Cola?[17] Bob Ryan wrote in his *Boston Globe* column that "Michael Jordan has been in danger of losing touch with the Real World for a long time," and he threatened to tarnish "the very image Nike is paying so dearly to exploit." Nike should tell Michael to "Do the Right Thing," Ryan believed, because "nothing he's said indicates he has a clue."[18]

An especially bitter attack came from Mark Kriegel's column in the *New York Post*. Jordan and Barkley, Kriegel charged, played not for the United States, but "for Nike, the Tammany gangsters of the sportsworld." After all, "Gangsters are loyal to the dollar too." Kriegel said he respected the public protest against racism by the U.S. African-American athletes at the 1968 Olympics: "Theirs was an act of politics, an act of courage, and an act of significance." Now Jordan and Barkley were making statements, "But not about racism. Not about anything really. Just about Nike, a company which has learned, above all else, how to sell $150 sneakers to [poor African-American] kids on Saratoga Avenue." "What a bunch of bums," Kriegel concluded.[19]

The stakes were huge. An estimated audience of six hundred million in 193 countries would be watching the basketball finals. As criticism rose, a Nike director tried to distance the company from the controversy. "We've had no conversations with Michael this week," went the strange announcement, "and we won't." Privately, Knight was said to be appalled by the terrible publicity.[20] When, however, the Dream Team marched to the stand to receive their gold medals before a watching world, Jordan had solved the problem. He draped himself in the U.S. flag and so hid the Reebok emblem. "I stood up for what I believed in," he announced. After all, "When you hire 12 Clint Eastwoods to do a job for you, you don't ask them what bullets they're going to be putting in their gun." "If I offended anybody," Jordan declared, "too bad."[21]

His reputation, already tarnished for associations with gamblers and drug dealers, was not enhanced. The shoe companies nevertheless seemed to profit. "Now everybody looks at the Olympics as Nike vs. Reebok," one sports analyst noted. "The companies brag about who's going to wear what, when, and the networks go for it hook, line, and sinker."[22] Vulgar commercialization of the Olympics was not news. Other charges surfacing against Nike, however, were appallingly new.

## *"There's No Telling What Can Happen to the Business If China Truly Catches On"*

By the early 1990s, Nike had recovered from its errors in underestimating competitors and the importance of the women's shoe market. It dominated the sportswear, especially sneaker, business. Nike's $4 billion in annual revenue nearly doubled that of its closest competitor. Wieden & Kennedy's advertising remained fresh and successful. So did Phil Knight's courtship of sports luminaries: about seven times more athletes were under contract with Nike than with any other company. These Nike endorsers included eighty NBA players led by Michael Jordan. It seemed impossible to watch a major basketball, baseball, or football contest on U.S. or international television without being constantly confronted by the Swoosh. "Professional athletes," wrote correspondent Dan Weil, served "as moving billboards for Nike shoes and apparel." Soccer, the most popular of international sports, at least outside the United States, was another matter. As yet, Knight had shown little interest in this sport.[23]

In a revealing series of articles in 1996 on "globalization" and the new U.S. transnational corporation, the *Washington Post* believed that "No company symbolizes the mobilization of American companies overseas more than Nike Inc. Its 30-year history in Asia is as close as any one company's story can be to the history of globalization, to the spread of dollars—and [German] marks, and [Japanese] yen—into the poor corners of the earth." It was a story, the newspaper added, "of restless and ruthless capital continually moving from country to country in search of new markets and untapped low-wage labor."[24] Knight, of course, had discovered the value of Asia more than thirty years earlier—as a source of ideas for shoes, as a place to find money for expansion, as a vast potential market, and now especially as a production line where new transnationals could find efficient, extremely cheap labor.

Exploiting low-wage labor to produce high-quality goods for American and European markets was a telling characteristic of the new transnationals. Before the 1960s, traditional multinationals tended to make their quality products in the United States, Europe, or, at the end of the era, Japan. These nations had reputations for style and quality. Goods from Taiwan, Hong Kong, and South Korea, on the other hand, had a reputation for being cheap and badly made. In the 1970s and 1980s, executives such as Knight saw that with new technology—especially computers and faxes that allowed a U.S. corporation to control overseas plants second by second—production could be done nearly anywhere. And if that anywhere had cheap, disciplined labor, profits could skyrocket. Between 1988 and 1995, producers such as Nike and Reebok poured more than $400 billion into so-called developing countries where that cheap labor lived.[25]

Knight spied the opportunity earlier than most. His first shoes had come out of 1960s Japan, then a low-wage, highly efficient system. When Japanese labor became more expensive, Nike signed contracts with South Korean entrepreneurs. Some of the first Korean shoes made in 1975 are displayed in a glass case in Hur Kwang Soo's office in Seoul. Hur ransacked Seoul's markets that year to find soft leather and rubber for Nike's famous waffle sole. He was so successful that by the 1990s his plants turned out four million pairs of Nike shoes each year. By the 1990s, however, South Korea's laborers, like Japan's in the 1970s, demanded better wages and working conditions. Hur and other Nike contractors quickly set up plants in Southeast Asia where laborers were more passive. Between 1988 and 1992, South Korea's share of Nike's total production fell from 66 percent to 42 percent. But Hur, now with his own transnational firm working in Southeast Asia under contract to Nike, grew ever richer.[26]

Knight, always admiring of the Asian way of business, was direct about why Nike made high profits. "We were . . . good at keeping our manufacturing costs down," he told an interviewer in 1992. "Puma and Adidas were still manufacturing in high-wage European countries. But we knew that wages were lower in Asia, and we knew how to get around in that environment."[27] Some of his plans failed. The Philippines proved too full of bureaucrats and corruption, so Nike quickly pulled out. The business climate in Taiwan and Indonesia, on the other hand, was near perfect. Thailand also produced millions of pairs of shoes. Taiwanese technology was so good that Knight put a research lab for new, advanced products in the capital city of Taipei.

Then in 1978 China began to open up and welcome foreign investments. It quickly became obvious that this ever-growing population of 1.5 billion offered the potential for huge profits. Knight was enchanted by his first visit to the People's Republic of China in 1980. As Nike closed its two U.S. sneaker plants (in New Hampshire and Maine) in the 1980s and began to focus on production in Asia, Communist China appeared to be the door to long-term success and riches. Problems, however, quickly appeared.[28]

Nike had to work with factories owned by the Chinese Communist government that had no idea how to turn out Nike-quality products. For five years, China's factories encountered huge problems in making white shoes. As a Nike vice president put it, "We tried to make white shoes, but we couldn't do it. There was too much dirt."[29] Chinese Communist leaders, moreover, ruthlessly imprisoned or otherwise silenced dissenters, most notably by killing large numbers of them in Beijing's Tiananmen Square during early June 1989 when they demanded a more democratic system.

Ted Turner's CNN televised the early moments of the clash. Realizing CNN's power, Chinese authorities pulled the plugs on the network's equipment and sent its reporters packing. U.S. law stipulated that nations committing continuing human rights abuses were not to receive trading privileges in the American market. Nike and other producers who exported Chinese-made goods into the United States thus faced the prospect of those exports being reduced in 1992 when an angry U.S. Congress placed restrictions on trade. Only a veto of the bill by President George Bush averted a crisis between the Americans and Chinese. The problem nevertheless threatened to disrupt the two nations' relationship—and Nike's imports of low-cost products from China—as the Communists continued to arrest dissidents.

Still, the Chinese plants quickly passed North Korea's and Taiwan's to become Nike's fastest growing production source. The facilities in China were developed by South Korean and especially Taiwanese and overseas Chinese investors who understood how the Chinese governmental and family-oriented economic system functioned. In 1989, as Nike thankfully ended its last contract with plants owned by the Chinese government, the Tsai family from Hong Kong moved in to set up factories. Where the Tsais built factories on the Pearl River Delta had been home mostly to pigs and chickens. It was an area in which there was an hour wait to use the phone at the local telephone office. Within seven years, the Tsais' Yue Huen corporation, located among new high-rise apartments and a six-lane highway, employed 54,000 people making shoes for Nike, Reebok, and Adidas. Yue Yuen was the world's largest supplier for each of those companies and probably the largest foreign investment in booming South China.

By 1995, its ninety-seven production lines made forty-five million pairs of sneakers. The Tsais negotiated highly profitable deals with the local Chinese bureaucrats, deals allowing investors to bring in massive amounts of up-to-date equipment without levy. Yue Huen did this, moreover, while somehow keeping separate the production of Nike, Reebok, and Adidas shoes and not revealing secrets of one company to the others. Sports shoes have about two hundred parts. In a case study of brilliant vertical integration of production, the Tsais produced most of these materials internally, even down to the $2,000 shoe molds. Such integration, combined with cheap labor, climaxed in rich profit margins of 25 to 38 percent. Meanwhile, the Tsais planned to expand sneaker production in Indonesia and Vietnam. New York City's Goldman Sachs investment bank financed the expansion of the Hong Kong transnational into Southeast Asia.[30]

As the Tsais counted their profits, Phil Knight endured bitter criticism. He came under fire just as Michael Jordan was being scathingly attacked for his involvement in gambling and his lack of political involvement. In 1992, Nike, along with Sears and Levi Strauss, stood accused of allegedly selling goods made by Chinese prison labor. It is against U.S. law to import the products of such labor. The three American companies began spot-checking all their Chinese suppliers to ensure that prisoners were not involved. While these accusations died down, another did not: that Asian producers for Nike and other shoe companies paid near-slave wages to overworked employees who endured horrible working conditions.

Four Indonesian plants, owned by South Koreans, paid young girls as little as 15 cents an hour for an eleven-hour day. Nike shoes that cost $5.60 to make in Asia sold in the West for $70 and up. Michael Jordan's $20-million endorsement fee was higher than the combined yearly payrolls of the Indonesian plants that made the shoes. Nike's general manager in Indonesia countered that "they are low wages. But we've come in here and given jobs to thousands of people who wouldn't be working otherwise."[31] Other Nike executives argued that they did not have any actual supervision over Asian plants; the factories were built and operated by local families (such as the Tsais) to whom Nike contracted the work. These executives added that since competitors such as Adidas used this low-cost labor, Nike had to employ it if the company hoped to compete in world markets. But the charges did not go away, especially as human-rights organizations learned of Korean operators physically beating employees in the new Vietnam plants.

Knight and other investors liked to point out that the U.S. transnationals helped create a new, if small, Asian middle class. China's manufacturing wages rose by 27 percent in 1993 and 1994, and by 14.5 percent in 1995. These rates rose from a low base, but they did seem to offer hope, especially to Nike sales agents.[32] For if cheap labor provided large profit margins, 1.5 billion Chinese consumers could provide net profits beyond imagination. As *Public Relations Journal* phrased it in 1993: "Consumerism has arrived in China." If the Communist Party's drab uniforms symbolized China's past, "Nike sneakers, Big Macs, and Pierre Cardin suits are symbols of China's future."[33]

The vast nation was served by 1,700 daily and weekly

newspapers, extensive television was regularly available at least to 800 million Chinese (courtesy especially of Rupert Murdoch, Ted Turner, and the BBC), and an extensive network of sport sponsorships evolved—all ready and waiting for imaginative advertisers such as Nike. In the 1780s, 1840s, 1890s, and 1970s, overly imaginative Americans had falsely claimed that the great China Market was becoming a reality. In the 1980s and 1990s, two centuries of sometimes desperate hope finally seemed to be turning into reality.

Phil Knight captured the moment: "There's no telling what can happen to the business if China truly catches on."[34] He certainly did not intend, of course, to depend entirely on China. Nike's sales outside the United States in 1992 amounted to a billion dollars. Only 15 percent came from Asian countries, 75 percent from Europe. The remaining 10 percent came from Canada and Latin America. In 1991 European sales had doubled. The upsurge came even before Knight geared up to exploit the 1992 Olympics.[35] He obtained exclusive coverage for his products on the pan-European cable powerhouse, Eurosport. Ads featuring Michael Jordan ran on Eurosport and MTV Europe. Nike raised a spectacular one-hundred-square-foot mural of Jordan near Paris's Bercy Stadium. Wieden & Kennedy accordingly opened offices in Hilversum, a suburb of Amsterdam, so the agency could oversee Nike's European ads on the spot. One of the projects was expanding *Nike NBA Action Report,* a weekly recap of NBA games for foreign markets that naturally tended to feature Jordan. Converse had written a large check to the NBA so it would be called the league's "official sneaker," but fans around the world could be forgiven if they thought that Nike held that title.[36]

Two U.S. firms, Reebok and especially Nike, deployed

American advertising skills and technology to eclipse their once-powerful European competitors, Adidas and Puma. Spending upwards of $100 million each on advertising in Europe (while Adidas could muster only $60 million), the two U.S. giants surged from having a five-percent share of the European market in 1983 to a fifty-percent share in 1993. Meanwhile they enormously expanded that market. They also set styles. In Paris fashion shows, beautiful models strutted down runways with the latest dresses and canvas high-top sneakers. In Frankfurt, Germany, a leading rabbi was observed wearing his yarmulke and a long robe over Air Jordans as he attended a rally protesting violence by racist German "skinheads."[37]

## *"The Higher the Satellite, the Lower the Culture?"*

American "soft power," as its advocates proudly termed it, was now fully in view.[38] Soft power referred to the influence of U.S. culture and commerce, rather than to its military and political muscle. Transnationals such as Nike exemplified such soft power. Their influence was made greater by widespread use of the English language—the international language of computers, science, and many of the young who considered themselves "cool." By the 1990s, some 70 percent of Western Europeans ages eighteen to twenty-four spoke English. (Only 20 percent of those over fifty-five years of age, however, could read or speak the language.)[39] It was the young who idolized Jordan and the "Dream Team," and who bought sneakers and Chicago Bulls' clothing.

The transnational manufacturers also profited from continued spread of U.S. transnational communications. The ABC network bought into one of Germany's leading

television stations. ABC's highly successful sports sub-
sidiary, ESPN, controlled one-third of Europe's largest
sports network, Eurosport. The NBC network in the
United States meanwhile took over Superchannel, a cable
operation that reached sixty million Europeans. Only one
percent of prime-time American television shows were
produced overseas. But nearly 80 percent of Europe's
television programs originated in the United States. It was
an impressive exercise of soft power.[40]

The new American capitalism did not go unchallenged.
European critics claimed the networks were too parochial
and U.S.-oriented. Transnationals responded by featuring
European events while becoming more multilingual and
playing down local American stories. These responses did
not satisfy France's Minister of Culture, Jack Lang. He
believed the world should fear that "vast financial groups
and entertainment industries will impose cultural unifor-
mity on a a global scale [.]" Lang wondered, "Will technology enrich us . . . or might the truth be more ominous: the
higher the satellite, the lower the culture?" After all, he
added, "the disappearance of languages and cultural
forms is the great risk today. Diversity threatens to be
replaced by an international mass culture without roots,
soul, color, or taste."

Lang warned that soft power moved mostly in one
direction because Americans were so closed-minded and
provincial, if not grossly ignorant of other cultures. An
author from Latin America or Europe could find readers
more easily "in Moscow than in . . . Los Angeles. It is
much easier for a European filmmaker to be seen in
Tokyo than Atlanta." United States culture, this "immense
empire of profit," had become a "financial and intellectual
imperialism which no longer grabs territory, or rarely, but
grabs consciousness, ways of thinking, ways of living."
The French minister exclaimed: "We must act if tomor-

row we don't want to be nothing but the sandwich board of the multinationals."[41]

Advertisements of Nike and other U.S. corporations nevertheless flourished while their European sales boomed. The opposition of Lang and other critics caused not even a hiccup as American soft power continued to inundate foreign cultures. Rupert Murdoch's multinational operation in China, however, suffered a significant setback.

Murdoch bought Hong Kong's powerful Star TV. Nike, one of Star's initial advertisers, had beamed programs into fifty-three countries, including China. In a 1993 speech, Murdoch made the mistake of bragging that "Advances in the technology of communications have proved an unambiguous threat to totalitarian regimes everywhere." Satellite television could simply bypass state-run newspapers and television. Unfortunately for Murdoch, China's Communist government agreed with him. It quickly moved to keep Star's programs out of the country. The campaign even outlawed ownership of the dishes needed to receive Star's satellite signal.

Murdoch immediately surrendered. He replaced an objective BBC news program from London with Chinese-language films. He publicly declared that although "we Americans don't like to admit it . . . authoritarian countries can work." Ted Turner also got the message. The creator of CNN blasted the U.S. government for trying "to tell so many other countries in the world what to do" about human rights.[42]

During the early 1990s, Murdoch and Turner had learned much about how their political views could undermine their global economic empires. Nike and its subcontractors in Asia also came under intense fire for allegedly growing rich through the exploitation of poor workers. Michael Jordan meanwhile discovered in both the United States and at the Olympic Games in Spain how the media that enriched him could also be the media that wounded him before an international audience.

Phil Knight's ambition never diminished, regardless of the criticism. "I'd say we're only halfway to being truly global," declared this head of one of the most successful of all global companies. Jordan, however, began to bend under the never-ceasing attention and criticism.

# CHAPTER V

## *A Faustian Bargain*

On October 22, 1992, Michael Jordan was summoned to testify at the drug and money-laundering trial of James "Slim" Bouler. The media turned out en masse at the Charlotte, North Carolina, courtroom. Jordan's appearance began a year of triumph and tragedy that set his international fame off in new directions.

In a nine-minute appearance on the witness stand, he admitted lying to the press about his $57,000 check to Bouler, which had been discovered by federal authorities. Jordan had earlier said the check was merely a loan. Actually it was payment for golf, poker, and other debts piled up over an October 1991 three-day weekend of nonstop gambling. He lied, Jordan declared, because he wanted "to save the embarrassment and pain" of such a "connection to gambling." In other words, he did not want his vast public to understand what he had done. The U.S. Attorney intended neither to investigate the star nor embarrass him on the witness stand. The attorney knew that tough questioning could anger the jury from Jordan's home state, where he remained hugely popular.[1]

Days later, he stood at the one place where, he always

said, he felt most comfortable and secure: midcourt where cameras, satellites, and cable flashed his image to millions as another NBA season got underway. In their quest for a third straight championship, a feat not accomplished since Bill Russell's Boston Celtics' triumphs of a quarter-century earlier, the Bulls had little trouble winning their division and reaching the playoffs. Nor did Jordan have problems winning his seventh straight scoring title. In the first round of the playoffs, the Bulls disposed of Cleveland. In the conference finals, however, they lost the first two games against their hated rivals, the New York Knicks.

Just before the second loss, reporters discovered that Jordan had spent the late afternoon and night before the game gambling at an Atlantic City casino. He had supposedly lost $5,000 in a private pit the casino thoughtfully set aside for him. One witness claimed to have seen him at the gambling tables as late as 2:30 A.M., a charge Jordan heatedly denied. He insisted he was back in New York City and in bed by 1:00 A.M., so had plenty of sleep for Game Two—in which he scored 36 points in the losing effort. Jordan's father, acting as his spokesman, argued that his son had the right, indeed the need, to relax during the pressure-packed playoffs. Coach Phil Jackson agreed. Jordan could hardly sit in his hotel room for twelve hours, and because of his fame, the coach noted, "He can't go anywhere in Manhattan. So if he went down there [to Atlantic City] I felt perfectly comfortable."[2]

Much of the press, led by columnist Mike Lupica, also defended Jordan's right to some privacy. Quoting columnist Bob Greene's line that "He's leading Elvis's life," Lupica declared that Jordan's critics "really need to shut up." For "Michael Jordan has been blessed with a talent for basketball the likes of which we will never see again. . . . He has spent a basketball life improving genius. Jordan didn't break the law . . . ," Lupica concluded. "He let no one down." Soon he "will get tired of all this and walk away, and it will feel like he took the whole sport with him."[3]

The walking away was closer than Lupica, and probably Jordan, realized. But the getting "tired of all this" was immediate. For the first time, the Bulls' star refused to talk to a press corps he believed had wronged him over the Atlantic City episode. "The great news media boycott of '93," as it was quickly dubbed, received full support from his teammates. His father handled all interviews. The NBA chiefs, however, were not pleased by Jordan biting the hands that fed them vast amounts of free advertising and lavish profits. Commissioner David Stern's office fined the Bulls $25,000 for ignoring the press. *New York Times* columnist William C. Rhoden condemned Stern's action: "The league's primary responsibility is to protect its players rights, not to preserve media privileges, especially when those privileges seem to invade personal lives and privacy."[4]

Rhoden was probably correct, or at least he was before the 1980s, when the NBA, led by Commissioner Stern and Michael Jordan, signed contracts to make millions of dollars by using the media for paid—and unpaid—advertising. The press, angered at Jordan's and the Bulls' boycott, now demanded its pound of flesh: access when and where the media desired. To live off the media opened the possibility of being damned by the media. Jordan and Stern had made an interesting Faustian bargain—that is, like the legend of the magician in medieval Germany who sold his soul to the Devil in return for knowledge and power, the NBA sold itself to the media for power and profit. Now the media demanded to receive its part of the bargain. As the Bulls, NBA, and media sparred, Chicago defeated the Knicks by 20 points in Game Three on the way to winning four straight games and the conference championship.

When the New York series ended, a book appeared from a San Diego sports executive, Richard Esquinas. He titled it, *Michael and Me: Our Gambling Addiction.* Esquinas claimed that in ten days of golf and card playing he had won $1.25 million from Jordan. Most of his winnings piled up, he claimed, when the star insisted on "chasing," that is, betting double-or-nothing. According to Esquinas, he was embarrassed to take so much money from Jordan and, at the basketball player's request, negotiated the amount down to $300,000. Jordan admitted he knew Esquinas, but pronounced the $300,000 figure to be "preposterous."[5]

In headlining Esquinas's charges, the media raised two highly troubling questions. The first: although Jordan piled up such debts and dealt with questionable characters, he claimed he never bet on basketball games. But, reporters speculated, when he owed operators such as "Slim" Bouler and Esquinas so much money, did they perhaps hint he could cut his debts by slipping them inside information about upcoming games?

The second question: leaving aside the issue of a possible addiction to gambling, it seemed obvious that Jordan had terrible judgment in choosing friends for golf and poker. Harvey Araton of the *New York Times* wrote, "From Jordan's public scorecard, we know of one gambling partner who was shot to death, another who's in prison, and a third who is apparently collecting a debt from Jordan by publishing a bet-and-tell-tome that has the [NBA] sweating out another Jordan scent of impropriety."[6] Famed *Chicago Tribune* columnist Mike Royko noted how Esquinas had apparently hustled Jordan into giving him strokes (a decisive advantage), then took his money on the golf course. Jordan had been so taken in, Royko believed, that this was not gambling—gambling meant taking a risk: "It sounds to me like Esquinas was taking about as much of a risk as a hawk does when it swoops down on a pigeon."[7]

Jordan answered the first question adamantly: he had never done anything to compromise his play or his commitment to basketball. The NBA investigated Esquinas's allegations, then again agreed that the star had done nothing to break league rules, especially rules outlawing betting on games. As for the second question, Jordan acknowledged he had to do better in choosing his friends and, especially, in playing golf with people he hardly knew.

The Bulls' leader finally broke his silence and talked to the media after the first game of the championship series against the Phoenix Suns. Chicago had won 100–92, while Jordan led all scorers with 31 points. The game drew one of the largest television audiences in NBA history, less because of Jordan's widely publicized scandals (although they doubtless drew some curious viewers), than because of a heralded matchup between Jordan and Suns' star Charles Barkley. Another famed endorser of Nike products, Barkley was determined to surpass the Bulls' star's commercial popularity by acting on court and in television ads as Jordan's opposite: a direct, tough-talking brawler.

Jordan took obvious pleasure in scoring crucial points as the Bulls defeated the Suns in six games. In Game Four, Jordan scored 55 points, including the decisive basket when he shot directly over Barkley. In the finals overall he shot often and well: his 41 points-per-game average set another NBA record.

As the final buzzer sounded, but before Jordan could join his teammates in celebration, a McDonald's advertising crew was on the court filming a commercial. The voice-over in the commercial said, "Michael, you've just won your third straight NBA championship. Are you hungry for a fourth?" A sweating, smiling Jordan replied, "I'm hungry for a Big Mac." Film footage was added from the final game showing Jordan flying to the basket for a lay-up. Within twelve hours the editing was finished. Within twenty-four hours the ad was fed by satellites to ESPN, MTV, and other cable networks, as well as into noncable networks. Jordan and the media had again profitably joined together through communication technology. Only when this job was done could Jordan celebrate.[8]

The Bulls had matched the great Celtic teams of the 1960s, while Jordan delighted in pointing out to the press that he had surpassed former greats Magic Johnson, Larry Bird, and Isiah Thomas, who had never won three consecutive championships. "This means I'm right up there with them . . . if not a step above." His competitive fire rose to full-flame: "I was looking to separate myself from Magic and Bird. They never did it. But I did."[9]

Jordan sounded a different note than he had several weeks before during his boycott of the media: "My love for the game is very strong now. And as long as the love is strong, I'm going to keep playing." Nike, McDonald's, and his many other endorsements were delighted to hear this. When these companies' officials were asked about the gambling problems, they emphasized that Jordan had their full support. To prove it, they cancelled none of his advertisements. Chicagoans certainly agreed with these companies. As Don Pierson wrote in the *Chicago Tribune,* to fully appreciate Jordan's global fame one had to have "a European perspective," for in Europe, "in cities he never has visited, billboards loom [with Jordan's face] with no identification necessary." As "for Chicagoans, Jordan's greatest contribution is he has displaced Al Capone as the city's most famous character. . . . The world's most visible athlete, he has brought new meaning to the word mob."[10]

John Skorburg, chief economist for the Chicagoland Chamber of Commerce, declared he "wouldn't be surprised" if Jordan's value to the region "approached a billion" dollars. At least four of the companies the star endorsed were based in the area, as were two of the large agencies that made commercials for them. Newspaper sales leaped up 30 to 50 percent during the championship series. The Bulls themselves had been valued at $18.7 million in 1985, but after eight years of Jordan the franchise was now estimated to be worth close to $200 million. Especially notable was his pull on overseas businesspeople who looked for headquarters and meeting sites in the United States. As one Illinois state official observed, "When we attend international trade shows to sell the city and state overseas, one of the first things people ask is, 'Do you have any posters of Michael Jordan?' "11

The Bulls' star seemed to have climbed back to the peak of the basketball and business worlds. This ascent of 1992–1993, however, had been made treacherous by the gambling allegations and the revelations about some of his off-court associations. In a 1988 interview, Jordan recounted that he suffered nightmares in which he made a mistake and destroyed his reputation. Especially fearful of accusations of drug-taking or alcoholism, he was determined to stay far away from both. "They're nightmares of something terrible happening to me that would destroy a lot of people's dreams or conceptions of me—that's the biggest nightmare I live every day."

## Tragedy

During the night of July 22–23, 1993, James Jordan drove from Wilmington, North Carolina, to Charlotte, where he planned to take a plane to Chicago to see his son. In 1985,

James and especially Deloris Jordan had already become so busy traveling to make money for themselves (notably from television ads in which Deloris starred) or to help Michael that they had moved to Charlotte to be near a major airport. James pulled off Route 74 to sleep. Two eighteen-year-olds approached to rob him, then shot him once through the chest. He apparently died instantly. When the two killers searched the victim's belongings and discovered who he was, they panicked. They drove the car thirty miles across the South Carolina border and dumped the body in a swamp. The two then aimlessly drove the car for three more days before ditching it in Fayetteville, North Carolina. A fisherman found the badly decomposed body on August 3. It was quickly identified as James Jordan. Authorities then linked the body with the deserted car.

The new technology and media again moved to center stage in Michael Jordan's life. The two killers had used the car's cellular phone to make calls. Unlike regular phones that usually depend on copper wires to carry calls, cellular calls are transmitted in the open by radio signals. Their source and destination are easy to trace through the carrier companies that provide the service. Larry Martin Demery and Daniel Andre Green were quickly arrested for the murder. Demery was already under indictment for armed robbery. Green had just been paroled after serving less than two years for assault with a deadly weapon with intent to kill. He had also been sentenced for armed robbery. The two men were waiting along the road for someone, anyone, to rob. It was, noted a North Carolina investigator, "the kind of random violence that all the public was . . . afraid of."[12]

Michael Jordan had grown close to his father. During the crises of the gambling charges, James had been Michael's spokesman. (Ironically, when the murder was first discovered, some in the media mistakenly guessed that it must somehow be linked with Michael's gambling associations.) At the funeral, the son held his composure until he left the church. He then broke down. Phil Knight, who had flown in from Nike's headquarters in Oregon, also began to cry. Knight looked at Jordan and thought, "Superman in tears."[13]

After mourning for several months, Jordan called a press conference on October 6, 1993. He dramatically announced his retirement from the Bulls. "I have nothing more to prove in basketball," he declared.[14] No one who followed the sport could disagree. But just four months earlier he had ardently professed his "love" for the game. To retire at his prime, when he was only thirty years old, and when the Bulls looked forward to a string of championships, led the well-informed to speculate that the gambling revelations, his father's death, and the incessant media crush that had grown to hot intensity in recent months had actually forced the decision.

## Baseball Interlude

Jordan's competitive urges, however, had not lessened. He needed challenges, public challenges, not merely those around the card table or on the golf course. He also needed public attention, especially for the benefit of his endorsements—although he wanted such attention on his terms. Soon after retiring from basketball, he told columnist Bob Greene of riding a bike with friends in California when they saw a pickup basketball game. Jordan got off his bike and joined the game. He told Greene that "pretty soon about six thousand people had gathered. So I finished the game and left." Jordan added it was a good moment: "I think we're going to re-create it for a commercial."[15]

The opportunities and competitive fire were too strong. He decided to try the sport that had once been his first love, baseball. He kept it in the family by signing with the Chicago White Sox, a club owned by his friend Jerry Reinsdorf, who also owned the Bulls.

Jordan and his fans quickly discovered he might not be Superman after all, at least not while wearing a baseball uniform. At the ballpark he more resembled Clark Kent. The White Sox sent him to Birmingham, Alabama, to a Double-A league two levels below the major leagues in talent, two-hundred light years below the major leagues in style. While Bulls and White Sox players dressed in plush clubhouses where meals were catered, then traveled sumptuously on chartered jets, Class AA ballplayers dressed in dank, small park dressing rooms, lived on tight allowances of meal money, and tried to get their sleep on grueling long-distance bus rides. Jordan often moved by private car, although he bought a new, luxurious bus for the team. Otherwise, he tried to fit in and pay his dues. This was difficult given that he was the most recognizable athlete in the world who earned millions of dollars each month ($1,200 from his baseball salary), while his teammates earned hundreds.

The Birmingham Baron games became hot tickets. The Barons' soaring attendance was not matched by Jordan's performance on the field. His speed and baserunning skills approximated big-league standards. But his hitting, especially against breaking pitches, and fielding sometimes fell below even Double-A standards. He hit a sad .202 while driving only three balls out of the park for home runs. At times, Jordan embarrassed himself. He knew the embarrassments were being shown by the nationally, indeed internationally, watched sports shows that were shadowing him from town to town. Bob Greene noted that *Sports Illustrated,* which two years earlier put him on the cover as Sportsman of the Year, now ridiculed Jordan with a story whose coverline read: "Bag It, Michael! Jordan and the White Sox are Embarrassing Baseball." Greene concluded that "Having used Jordan to sell magazines when his skills in one sport were superb, *Sports Illustrated* was attempting to sell a few more issues by making fun of his failings."[16] So went the Faustian bargain in the newly wired world.

Jordan could leave basketball, but he could not leave the media of the new information age. Nor did he and his corporate clients want him to leave this media. Nike's annual sales had swollen to more than $4 billion while profits exploded. Many of those profits were generated from the $18 million Nike paid Jordan each year for his endorsement. He moved into an office at Nike's headquarters in Beaverton, Oregon—the only other office on the floor where Phil Knight had his desk. Wieden & Kennedy designed a fresh series of radio and television spots for Jordan and Nike. Knight even released a new Air Jordan shoe that listed the star's NBA highlights on the outersole. Meanwhile, McDonald's happily continued to pay him $3 million each year, Sara Lee up to $4 million (for his Hanes ads), Wheaties up to $3 million, Gatorade $2 million, and Chicagoland Chevrolet dealers an undisclosed amount to tell the public about their products.[17]

These corporations had decided that even without basketball, Jordan stood alone as a salesman. "There will be other stars in the NBA," a marketing analyst observed, "but it will be hard to get someone who packages all that Jordan had." He was attractive, articulate, relaxed on camera, flashed a wonderful smile, and that was "in addition to what he did on the court." His (and the NBA's) marketing prowess became glaringly evident when Jordan stood alongside baseball stars to sign autographs. Major league baseball's owners remained in the Dark

Ages on questions such as player relations, the commissioner's power, profit-sharing with players and poorer teams, and notably national and international marketing. Jordan received "all the requests for autographs," one sports marketing expert noted, while the baseball stars were "not given the attention their talents are due."[18]

The Bulls figured out how even a retired Jordan could help them pull in fans. The team had a one-ton bronze statue of him sculpted so it could be placed at the main entrance of the new United Center. The statue displayed Jordan floating through the air as he prepared to slam the ball down through the basket. It was so lifelike that the statue even had hair under the arms and, of course, wore Nike shoes. As reporter Jeff Coplon noted, "There's something peculiar here . . . and then you realize that the statue is the spitting macro-image of the [Nike] sneaker logo: marketing becomes art, becomes marketing once more."[19] The line between basketball and the market, never clear since 1891, had long since disappeared.

For both the game and the market, the inscription on the statue's base was most appropriate:

MICHAEL JORDAN
CHICAGO BULLS
1984–1993
*The best there ever was.*
*The best there ever will be.*

Meanwhile, baseball as a game (as opposed to the marketing of it) was proving too much for Jordan. Experts gave him the benefit of the doubt: if he had played the game regularly in his teens and twenties, he might have developed the reflexes needed to hit a ninety-mile-an-hour breaking pitch or the instincts required to run bases successfully. In the 1994 Arizona Fall League, Jordan managed to hit only .252 against mostly rookie and minor-league pitchers. As their headline player struck out at the high rate of once every four times at bat, his team, the Scottsdale Scorpions, drove back and forth to the bank. With Jordan on board, Scottsdale alone accounted for 87 percent of the league's total attendance. So many callers suddenly wanted Scorpion caps that an extra person had to be hired just to handle those orders.

In 1994, some twelve months after he had retired from basketball, *Forbes* magazine announced that Jordan led the list of athletes with the highest incomes for the third straight year. His marketing prowess was undiminished—partly, no doubt, because his advertising spots played well on the nostalgia of the Bulls' great years, partly because of the media frenzy that followed him around the Alabama and Arizona ballparks. The frenzy required that he be accompanied by two beefy bodyguards even while he was resting in the dugout.[20]

As its sales surged toward the $5 billion mark, Nike also prospered. Phil Knight planned a massive international campaign that would make foreign buyers (who now accounted for one-third of the firm's sales) more important than the U.S. market. Given his global popularity, Jordan was an integral part of Knight's plans. But Nike was beset with problems which had less to do with sales than with public image—although as Knight and Jordan well knew, sales and image could sooner or later become two sides of the same coin.

Several years before, a group named The Made in the USA Foundation began a one-million-dollar advertising attack on Nike and other U.S.-headquartered firms that produced most of their products overseas. American labor deserved to receive preference, the Foundation announced, over poorly paid, child, or prison labor abroad. Its ads told readers to send their "old, dirty, smelly, worn-out Nikes" to Knight so the company would "come back home to the United States and start making shoes here once again." The Foundation charged that during the 1980s, 65,000 U.S. laborers had lost well-paying jobs when Nike and other shoe manufacturers began doing more production and assembly in Asian countries. Made in the USA also quoted press reports that Nike spent $5.95 to make a pair of shoes in Indonesia, where workers were paid 14 cents an hour, then sold the shoes in the United States for between $49 and $125.[21]

Nike hit back by again noting it did not directly hire and pay Asian workers. The company instead worked through contractors who, it declared, had to pay a country's minimum wage. Moreover, Nike announced it employed more American manufacturing workers (1,200 out of a total company workforce of 6,500 in the United States) than any other athletic footwear company. But the Foundation's charges obviously stung. By 1994, Nike television ads began to show Jordan and track champion Jackie Joyner-Kersee talking seriously to students and adults about the need to support local youth sports programs.[22]

As the charges were hurled back and forth, Jordan continued to be silent about labor and wage issues. He appeared more frequently at his Chicago restaurant to chat up customers, and even moved around area country clubs in a self-proclaimed mission to become an immortal gin rummy player. But he could escape neither the continued frustrations of baseball nor the growing allegations against Nike.

## The Return

The Arizona Fall League frustrations blended into a winter of following the Bulls as they won games in their splendid new United Center. Jordan seemed to be ready to leave, needing only an excuse to escape from baseball. Foolish owners and a myopic players' union provided that excuse when their fumblings led to a players' strike in 1994. The strike gave baseball a permanent black eye by cancelling the World Series. As the trouble staggered on into the early spring training days of March 1995, Jordan announced that the strike prevented him from working out so he could be a better player.

Seventeen months after leaving the Bulls, he told the world he was returning. The NBA season was in its final months, but Jordan's impact was awesome, especially on the sport's business side. His first game against the Indiana Pacers turned into, as Coach Phil Jackson described it, "a three-ring circus, which was broadcast worldwide and attracted the largest TV audience of any regular season NBA game in history." Larry Brown, the Pacers' coach, captured the mood by declaring, "The Beatles and Elvis are back." When a film crew actually began zeroing in on Jordan's Nikes, one observer declared, "Now they're interviewing his shoes."[23]

Jordan was rusty. He missed too many shots as the Bulls lost in overtime. Tabloid headlines charged that "Air Jordan" had become only "Fair Jordan." A week later, however, he defeated Atlanta by scoring 32 points, including a long jump shot just as the final buzzer sounded. Then he scored 55 points to sink the New York Knicks, 113–111, in a media-splashed event at Madison Square Garden. Usually 100 to 150 media representatives covered Knicks' games. On this night, some 350, from a dozen countries, showed up—so many that not enough seats could be found. Scalpers sold $95 seats for $1,000. The game, shown on Ted Turner's cable station, drew an increasingly larger audience as the evening progressed until it hit a record number of viewers for cable broadcast of a basketball game.[24]

The Bulls lacked the cohesion to win another title. While Jordan had been away, they had consistently won. But there were no championships in 1994 or in 1995 after Jordan reappeared late in the season. A young Orlando team defeated them in the early playoffs. Not, however, without arousing a marketing mania. McDonald's celebrated Jordan's return with a set of television ads that featured him with other NBA stars. When he came back to the Bulls, he wore the number 45 on his uniform, instead of his old, now retired, 23—a change that ignited sales of Bulls jersey No. 45. In the Orlando series, one opponent who had guarded Jordan told the press that he was slower and "not the same as No. 23." In the next game, Jordan switched back to 23 and scored 38 points. The Bulls won, but Orlando complained about the uniform change—as, Coach Jackson noted, did a large number of parents who had bought No. 45 jerseys for their children. No league rule prohibited the change of number. But marketing principles and public relations posed real problems. The NBA fined the Bulls $100,000 for allowing Jordan to switch. Meanwhile, sales of No. 23 Bulls jerseys again took off.[25]

Jordan, despite the baseball interlude, remained an immensely profitable commodity in a society that, especially with the end of the Cold War, seemed to value profit, celebrity, and marketability above all else. He and Nike thus became post–Cold-War symbols—indeed phenomena—of American culture, American globalization, American marketing, American wealth, American-headquartered media, American-based transnationals. Jordan and Nike were also becoming symbols for the sometime corruption of this Americanization, when its too often seamy underside contaminated its professed principles.

The power of the new, post-1970s technology lay here:

while creating unimagined wealth more rapidly than ever before, it could also raise fundamental questions about the society that generated that wealth. It could raise such questions more rapidly and intensely, and to billions of more viewers, moreover, than ever before.

# CHAPTER VI

## *"The Greatest Endorser of the Twentieth Century" or "An Insidious Form of Imperialism"?*

In 1995 Michael Jordan felt bitter about losing in the playoffs. He was almost equally incensed over the arrival of young players in the NBA who were undisciplined, insensitive, overpaid, immature, and concerned more about their personal statistics than team success. He especially noted these *nouveaux riches* did not pay proper respect to their already proven elders. His views resembled those held by Magic Johnson, Larry Bird, and Isiah Thomas toward himself in 1984.

Stories, planted by both reporters and some younger players, circulated that Jordan's championship days were over. It was time for him to pass on the torch of NBA leadership, and also pass on the fabulously profitable business deals that came with that torch. During the summer of 1995, Jordan therefore pushed himself through a terrifyingly rigorous conditioning program. He also worked hours each day on his jump shot. He knew he had lost a half-step, and that he could no longer slash to the basket with the speed that had set him apart. "Beating defenses this way [by shooting over them] is just as enjoyable as the other way." he decided.[1] He somehow retooled his

game even while filming the movie *Space Jam.* Jordan
starred with actor Bill Murray and popular cartoon figures to win a climactic basketball game. This highly successful film scored $230 million at the box office and over
$200 million more in video sales.

His shooting proved to be equally successful as the season began. He won his eighth scoring title in 1995–1996
with a 30.4 per-game average. A television analyst noted
Jordan's two-way domination: "Line up all the players in
the league and ask them which player they'd least want to
guard, and which player they'd least want to guard them,
and in almost every case the answer would be Michael
Jordan."[2] In superb shape, he started all eighty-two
regular-season games. He aimed not only to win but at
times to destroy an opponent mentally. "I just want to get
inside their head," he declared. "Like when I'm playing
against a rookie, I might say: 'You watched me on TV,
now you're going to see me for real. [But] on TV you can
change the channel; you can't now."[3]

Bulls General Manager Jerry Krause acquired Dennis
Rodman, who, despite a passion for tattoos, changeable
multicolor hair, and various body piercings, was also the
NBA's best rebounder. Pippen had another outstanding
season. The Bulls broke all NBA records by winning
seventy-two games while losing only ten. Jerry West, a
Hall-of-Fame player, and now the general manager who
had built the Los Angeles Laker championship teams,
announced that "Michael Jordan is just the best ever."[4]

In the playoffs, Chicago swept by Orlando and New
York. The championship series against Seattle was broadcast to 175 countries in two dozen languages. The Bulls
won in six games. A tearful Jordan told reporters that the
final victory "happened on Father's Day, which makes it
even more special. There's no way to really describe it."[5]
He also won his fourth NBA Most Valuable Player award.

After enduring all the frustrations of playing baseball, Jordan again set the standard in basketball. One interesting standard could be measured by noting that in 1989–1990, six NBA players had shaved heads. Jordan then shaved his. By 1996, seventy-six players followed his example.[6] Jordan and the Bulls also set the standard in the 1996–1997 season for victories as they breezed into the playoffs. Phoenix Coach Danny Ainge had played with and admired Larry Bird when both were members of the championship Boston Celtics. "I always thought that Larry worked harder than any player . . . ," Ainge declared. "And . . . I never thought that Michael, or anyone, could ever be as intense as Larry in terms of winning. But Michael is at least his equal in all those categories, besides being the superior athlete." Ainge concluded, "Michael's the best player, without question, of all time."[7]

Jordan's intensity appeared in the championship series against the Utah Jazz and their star, Karl Malone, who had narrowly defeated Jordan to win the NBA's Most Valuable Player award. The Bulls' star scored 31 points to dominate Game One, including the winning long jump shot as the final buzzer sounded. Chicago went on to dominate the entire series.[8]

In 1998, the Bulls repeated their triumph over Utah to win a sixth championship. Again Jordan made the crucial points, including the decisive jump shot in the last eighteen seconds of the final game, which the Bulls won 87–86. This season, however, had a notably bittersweet flavor. There was an increasing feeling that this marked the last time Jordan, Pippen, and Coach Phil Jackson would be together. As Jordan played his season-ending games at various NBA cities, ticket brokers were able to charge as much as $200 per ticket so sentimental fans could wish him good-bye. Jackson announced his retirement. After the final championship game, Jackson and Jordan embraced at midcourt while whispering to each other. "I said," the coach told reporters, "it was just a magical ending, and that I don't know how much more a person can do in this game."[9]

Jordan had become an even more mythic figure. He moved well above the normal run of humanity even as much of that humanity tried to identify with him. "In a world hungry for public men and women to respect and admire," columnist Bob Greene wrote, "Jordan had come along to fill some need many might not even have been aware they fostered."[10]

## Expanding the Empire

Greene was correct. And nearly everyone who had been pulled into Jordan's orbit had been sucked in by television. He and his times were perfectly matched, Mike Lupica observed, because "we're—like it or not—members of the highlight generation. Our sports are geared to quick bursts," perfect for the leisurely television viewer with a short attention span. Julius Erving may have been as original as Jordan, but only those "who saw [Erving] in the [American Basketball Association] arenas [of the 1970s] remember his basketball skywriting." Expanded television, built on new technologies, "is the only reason that so much of what Jordan did in the NBA seemed so new," Lupica believed.[11]

Jordan's return had an electric effect on NBA television ratings for Ted Turner's cable network. In 1995–1996, those ratings shot up 21 percent over those of the year before. The fifteen Bulls games that were telecast attracted 50 percent more viewers than non-Bulls games. As one Turner broadcaster phrased it, Jordan "eats a tunafish sandwich and you get a 4.5 rating"—that is, twice the usual television audience for basketball. Such figures made it possible for Phil Knight to announce that "Michael Jordan is the greatest endorser of the 20th century."12

In 1997, the Great Endorser's earnings shot up to $100 million, or about 90 percent over those of 1996. The possibilities seemed endless. In addition to Nike, McDonald's, Oakley Sunglasses, Gatorade, Wilson Sporting Goods, Wheaties, Rayovac Batteries, and a half-dozen other companies, he was profiting from the *Space Jam* film, CBS-Fox Home Videos, WorldCom, and CBS Sports-Line—all products of the post-1970s technology. The CBS SportsLine deal put Jordan on the World Wide Web for ten years (for $10 million), to answer e-mail, analyze games, and, of course, do commercials.13

The arrangement worked out by Jordan's agent, David Falk, with WorldCom especially intrigued. WorldCom was the fourth largest long-distance phone company, with ardent ambitions to be number one. Jordan was to be WorldCom's launchpad to the top. All of the other products endorsed by Jordan, a WorldCom executive believed, would be advertised and hooked together in the company's commercials and web sites. Jordan could profit handsomely. As one observer put it, Falk "figures Jordan might persuade WorldCom to insert McDonald's coupons in its mailings, or get Sara Lee Coach leather-goods . . . to promote sales of backpacks by offering samples of Bijan Fragrances' Michael Jordan perfume."14 Imagine: because of the new late-twentieth-century media, a computer owner, filling some personal need the owner might not even be aware of having (as Bob Greene had phrased it), could—in a fit of impulse buying with just one click of the mouse—order everything Michael Jordan had pronounced good.

NBA Commissioner David Stern's most extravagant

dreams were coming true. Thus Stern's "manifest-destiny regime," as author Jeff Coplon termed it, raised the number of countries viewing weekly NBA games from 35 in 1986 to more than 175 ten years later.[15] The games went out over communication satellites in forty languages. Nowhere overseas did these satellites make Michael Jordan more famous than in the world's most populous, and potentially most profitable, country: China.

As Chinese from all walks of life stopped to watch the Bulls defeat Utah in the 1998 championship series, the cry of "Qiao Dan, Qiao Dan," or "Jordan, Jordan," was heard in the dormitories of Beijing University. One management major at the university said flatly that "Jordan is much more famous than [President] Clinton here." When a Chinese firm asked a thousand people to name the best-known Americans, Jordan finished second (just behind Thomas Edison by a narrow margin), and ahead of Albert Einstein, Mark Twain, and Bill Gates. On the avenues, vendors sold Michael Jordan posters and calendars alongside those of the late Chairman Mao, father of the Chinese Revolution. The Bulls' final playoff game against Utah drew such an audience that state television ran it three times. A week later, President Clinton made his first state visit to Beijing. A thirteen-year-old boy, Chen Tong, stood by the parade route to see the President's car, but told a reporter that while he liked "President Clinton, I even worship him," the other two Americans he held in reverence were "George Washington and Michael Jordan."[16]

As Beijing stores demonstrated, sales of NBA clothing soared parallel with the increased number of global viewers. The NBA was not making much money from anything with Jordan's likeness on it. Falk and the star had stopped those sales by threatening to take the NBA to court. Stern and the NBA backed off; they could make money in other ways. With Chicago's renewed championship run, for example, Bulls jackets became a fashion in Sweden.

The market was expanding so fast that in 1997 Jordan announced he was creating his own exclusive line of clothing. With financial backing from Phil Knight's Nike, the Jordan line was projected to take in $250 million in gross revenues during its first year—a figure that immediately made it one of the nation's largest clothing businesses. Jordan was drawn to the new venture for many reasons. He could run his own manufacturing and distributing company (with, that is, considerable help from Nike experts). As Jordan publicly mulled over the possibility of retiring from the NBA, moreover, being head of this business and overseeing the sale of Air Jordan sneakers could absorb some of his energy. "I wanted to invest in something that will keep me in touch with the game and the fans whenever I leave," he declared. "But I didn't want to do the ordinary, like coach or report from the sidelines. I want to leave my mark without actually having to be anywhere near the court."[17] The game that made him would not be the game that would hold him. The new global technology held out too many other opportunities for that.

Another reason for his new venture: he continued to be troubled by, and criticized for, the violence sometimes caused by adolescent passions for Air Jordan sneakers. "I don't want kids killing for these things," he reiterated. He was convinced that any change had "to start with parents instilling values in their kids that don't allow them to be so materialistic." Somewhere in his mind, Jordan must have known that such a hope was not likely to be realized very fully in an America full of television advertising, demands by parents and children for instant gratification, and, of course, the combined efforts of cultural icons like

Michael Jordan and overpowering technology to convince viewers to buy more and ever more. He consequently decided to produce clothes that were in colors street gangs usually had no interest in, and Air Jordans that would cost under $100.[18]

In mid-1998, *Fortune* magazine estimated that Jordan had at least a $10-billion impact on the U.S. economy. About half, or $5.2 billion, benefited Nike. Another $3.1 billion of increased sales of NBA-licensed clothing (especially jerseys with No. 23 on them) had passed through cash registers since Jordan had entered the league. *Fortune* also credited him with providing hundreds of millions of dollars in profit to television and cable companies.[19]

But the $10 billion only involved the United States. His true reach was global. It even included France, which had been fighting a losing battle throughout the twentieth century to keep American business and culture from penetrating its society. Until the mid-1990s, the blasé French had so studiously ignored the world's greatest endorser that Paris was one of the few cities in the world where Jordan could eat in a restaurant in peace. Then in mid-1997, the Bulls came to the French capital to play two games. A thousand journalists and France's prime minister attended. In the country that had led the attack since the 1920s, and especially in the 1980s and 1990s, on the expanding reach of U.S. culture and advertising-marketing, hard-bitten journalists, as well as thousands of fans, showed up in Bulls warm-up jackets. One of the reporters again demanded to know whether it was true that Jordan was a god. "I play a game of basketball," he explained. "I try to entertain for two hours and then let people go home to their lives. . . . I could never consider myself a god."[20]

It was fitting that Jordan climaxed the visit by posing under the Eiffel Tower wearing Nikes and promoting

McDonald's. Beneath an industrial wonder of the nineteenth century posed three wonders of the post-industrial era. The Eiffel Tower was one of the few sites Jordan could visit. The media that had made him now prevented him from taking his wife and three children out of their hotel room for fear of being mobbed by Parisians fanatical about the *taureau rouge.*

Germany had surrendered to the NBA-Jordan magic at least as early as 1992 when the U.S. Olympic Dream Team dominated television screens. One German basketball coach recalled that after the Olympics, ten to thirty kids called each day to ask where they could learn to play basketball. Then came an onslaught of NBA marketing and Nike television commercials. Soccer remained the nation's first sport (as, indeed, it remained throughout the world). But the 200,000 Germans playing basketball in the late 1990s doubled the number of ten years before. A German professional team won the European championship in 1993, then began selling its clothing by using NBA marketing techniques. But because of Jordan and television, NBA goods accounted for 20 percent of sales in several major outlets. "Basketball is a symbol for the American way of life, like American music, Whoppers, Big Macs, basketball jackets and caps," observed one German official.[21]

Europe was a special target, but not the only region targeted by Jordan-inspired basketball and marketing. In South Africa, Chicago Bulls hats appeared in cricket fields and also in Bushman villages. (Large street gangs, who learned about Americans from *Rambo* movies as well as television ads, called themselves "The Young Americans" and "The JFKs.") When South African officials warned that in such post-colonial societies as theirs the people could both admire—but also deeply resent—colonial power, an American replied that it was the British who had colonized South Africa. The United States had not done so. "Oh, yes you did," came the answer. "Culturally you did."[22]

In Japan, where many parts of U.S. culture had long been admired and absorbed, not only was basketball growing in importance, but a strange mania set in for old, beaten-up Nikes and Adidas. Nikes from the early 1970s fetched as much as $2,600 for one pair. Early Air Jordans gained popularity as buyers offered as much as $600 for mid-1980s models.[23]

The ability of basketball, U.S. advertising techniques, and American-dominated media to penetrate other cultures amazed observers. Christine Ockrent, a French television personality, believed that "The only true pan-European culture is the American culture." Historian Richard Pells, a close student of American culture's impact abroad, noted how European intellectuals worked to try to absorb the influence of "Hollywood and Hemingway, Elvis Presley and Michael Jordan," so they would become European as well as American icons.[24]

Such influence could be mind-bending, even forcing different generations to follow different paths. A senior official of Morocco's government, for example, said he was sending his children to U.S. schools instead of French institutions (in which he had been educated), for two reasons: "First, in the world we are going into if you don't speak English, you're illiterate. Second, the French system teaches you to be an administrator. The American system teaches you how to survive on your own. That's what I want my kids to know." The Moroccan official formed these impressions not only from direct contacts with Americans, but from U.S. television and films.[25]

Many observers argued that the power of American culture did not simply roar down a one-way street. Other nations might be seduced by parts of that culture, but they fiddled with and integrated it into their own dominant culture, whether European, Asian, or South African. Americans, these observers concluded, thus had to adapt to customs and beliefs in other nations if they hoped to sell McDonald's and Nikes. If the Americans did not adapt, they could be threatened with violent protests—as happened to Kentucky Fried Chicken when farmers in India saw the U.S. company as threatening their own small businesses. Cultural officials and intellectuals in France and elsewhere meanwhile tried to discourage, even outlaw, the use of English and the spread of some American culture.

One U.S. analyst concluded that while such a dynamic culture did not simply take over supposed "passive and vulnerable" countries, "it is certainly true that the major diffusionary source of this culture is a single Western country: the United States."[26] In other words, U.S. culture changed other cultures more than those cultures changed how Americans lived, thought, and spent their leisure time. One of Michael Jordan's most profitable endorsements was McDonald's, and one of the more interesting—if exaggerated—descriptions of how this culture affected other societies was offered by Ronald L. McDonald, in an authorized history of McDonald's:

> We have seen radical changes in the dining habits of Europeans that have been just as dramatic as the changes in their diets. In countries such as Austria, Switzerland, and Germany, the once popular wurst sandwiches, spicy sausages served in a French bread roll, didn't stand a chance against an All-American burger once it entered the market. Street vendors folded like houses of cards once the big American burgers appeared on the scene.

A more considered analysis was given by Richard F. Kuisel, who has written one of the best accounts of U.S.

cultural power (well entitled, *Seducing the French: The Dilemma of Americanization*). Kuisel encapsulated the transforming force of the new U.S. capitalism:

> What is important is that it seems European eating habits have been modified by fast food introduced by McDonald's. The disappearance of thousands of cafés in Paris as well as the long family lunch amounts to significant social change. Wearing sneakers, no matter how they are advertised, represents a new informality in European dress and perhaps even behavior. Watching MTV, even if it has been customized for European consumption, suggests that European youth are receiving social and cultural messages as Americans do. And children's imaginations are changed by viewing American television and Hollywood movies.

Kuisel quotes the greatest French statesman of the 1940 to 1970 era, Charles de Gaulle, as observing that "Great Britain is an island, France the cape of a continent, America another world." The United States itself, Kuisel concludes, did not have to change its own process of "Americanization" as it so dramatically changed other cultures.[27]

Friends closer than the French were bitterly protesting this "Americanization." Canadian historian Geoffrey Smith believed that "[I]n most global sport—so much of it Americanized—we behold a new and insidious form of imperialism." This "imperialism" was especially insidious for its "absurd monetary stakes" and its attractiveness to "millions around the globe." "[K]ids in Berlin and Madagascar" change local habits and "pay homage to Michael Jordan and the Chicago Bulls from head (bald) to foot (Nike)." Star basketball, hockey, and baseball players leave their home countries to play before the global media centered in the United States. "Small wonder," Smith believed, "that as free-trading international capital-

ism threatens the existence of traditional political struc-
tures, sports products and [sports] prodigies take on huge
importance."[28]

It should be remembered that while "Americanization"
had been seen as threatening to Canadians, Europeans,
and others since at least the 1920s (if not the 1890s when
basketball was invented), it had only recently taken on a
new and staggeringly powerful form. In 1984, when a fan
turned on television to watch the young Michael Jordan,
he probably watched on one of the three major networks
(NBC, CBS, ABC), because there were few other channels. To pull in the game even from those few networks,
the viewer needed either an antenna on the set or a hook-
up to the newly introduced cable lines. When Jordan
returned to win the NBA championships in 1996–1998,
the fan lived in quite another technological world. Ted
Turner and Rupert Murdoch carried games on their own
channels that sucked audiences away from the three old
networks. The new channels exploited communication
satellites and more powerful cable.

Turner, Murdoch, and Michael Eisner (who headed the
vast Walt Disney empire that owned ABC network, ESPN
sports channels, the Anaheim Angels baseball team, and
enjoyed extensive overseas access) no longer thought in
terms of just one product (as basketball) and one country
(as the United States). They saw the whole world as their
market, a market tied together by satellites. They then put
together mammoth marketing machines that used basketball (or baseball) games to show advertising that sold their
transnational corporation's books, movies, and other television programs.

The magic words were "packaging" and "synergy" (that
is, the cooperative working together of two or many more
goods to make much larger profits than the goods could
make alone). Michael Jordan again stood apart as a global

symbol of synergy's magic. He and his agent, David Falk, had begun in the 1990s to use a global communications company for selling not just one of the products Jordan endorsed, but a bundle of them linked together. Thus Jordan could suggest that his fans watch the *Space Jam* film while sitting in their Hanes underwear, eating Big Macs, washing those down with Gatorade, and preparing to buy Jordan's videos over their Jordan-endorsed cell phone.[29]

American media, advertising, and marketing entered an unexplored, unimagined era. It was an era that not only expanded "Americanization," but produced—even among some of the United States' historic friends—strong anti-Americanism. Michael Jordan personified that new era. So did Phil Knight.

## The Swooshifying of the World

Wearing his Nikes, Jordan's image flew around the world and across geographical boundaries that seemed increasingly to be—especially for the media that carried that image—almost meaningless lines on maps. Knight accurately proclaimed that "Sports has become the dominant entertainment of the world."[30] He stepped up his drive to make Nike the most powerful company in all sports. But the firm's sales dipped shortly after 1996 as shoe styles changed and sneakers began to fall out of favor. Critics charged that, in his drive to rule the market, Knight had overreached.

He indeed had paid millions of dollars to have the Swoosh placed on the athletic uniforms of ten NBA teams, more than forty universities, eight National Football League squads, and eight National Hockey League clubs. Knight also exploited the rising popularity of women's basketball, notably the 1996 U.S. Olympic team and its star, Sheryl Swoopes, who had her own Air

Swoopes shoe. Nike paid more attention to women's sports after women outspent men in purchasing athletic footwear for the first time in 1994, $5.4 billion to $5.3 billion.

U.S. women's groups, led by author Alice Walker and Congresswoman Maxine Waters (D-Calif.), told Knight his new attention to them was quite insufficient. American women wore Nikes to perform well, they told him, while "Indonesian, Vietnamese, and Chinese women making the shoes often suffer from inadequate wages, corporal punishment, forced overtime, and/or sexual harassment."[31]

Knight ran into more trouble when he overcame his old reluctance and bought the rights to pin the Swoosh on nine national soccer teams, including the world-famous Brazilian squad. He handed out $200 million over ten years to have the Brazilians, favored to win the 1998 World Cup, wear Nikes. Knight was targeting not only the tremendous global soccer audience, but the growing number of Hispanic-Americans and other soccer fanatics in the United States itself. France, however, not Brazil, won the World Cup in 1998. And Pelé, once the world's greatest and most famous soccer player and now Brazil's sports minister, blasted Nike's money for corrupting Brazil's leading sport. Nike dismissed the fight as merely one between Brazilian politicians, but the charges stung.[32]

Nike was condemned even in the sport that had given birth to Phil Knight's empire, track and field. As the official outfitter of the 1996 U.S. track and field team in the Olympics, Nike designed track suits with Swooshes instead of stars in the American flag. Condemned by *Newsweek* as "crass even by Olympic . . . standards," the uniform was finally ditched because of rules that limited the number of such logos on a uniform.

Despite these blistering criticisms and setbacks in the

mid-1990s, Knight determined to accelerate the company's global activities. In addition to sponsoring international soccer, he organized world championships of various types. The first Nike "Hoop Heroes" contest occurred in Japan during September 1996. It starred Jordan, Charles Barkley, and other Nike endorsers challenging wildly popular, three-hundred-pound Japanese sumo wrestlers to a game of basketball. Tickets sold out in twenty minutes. Acting like the powerful transnational it was, Nike controlled every part of the planning, advertising, and marketing. Knight set up a global marketing division to create similarly profitable sports events that would showcase Nike products worldwide. Not only was Nike now dominating sportswear sales, it was creating sports (Michael Jordan versus sumo wrestlers?) and the events at which the clothing would be peddled.[33]

The company already controlled 36 percent of the world market for sports equipment. Knight determined to tighten that grip not only by dreaming up international sports events, but by simply purchasing foreign companies. Nike thus took over the famous Canadian firm of Canstar Sports, which had established businesses around the world to sell its popular hockey equipment. Nike also plugged into vast computer systems. At first, Knight considered buying a television network, but, as Nike marketing executive Liz Dolan put it, "Who needs TV when you have the Internet?" The Nike website was planned to work like a television network, only it would be global immediately and open to commercial opportunities that were missing on television channels. Nor would Internet regulations be nearly as bothersome for Nike's highly imaginative advertising and marketing people.[34]

Thus Knight planned to supplement, if not replace, the new media of global television with the newer, hotter, more open, and more unregulated media of the Internet.

Such innovation could not, however, protect him and Nike from withering criticism for their purchasing of athletes, even universities, and for using mistreated Asian laborers in their shoe factories. Such criticism, it was to be noted, came almost entirely from angry private citizens, not from governments. The governments, including the U.S. government, said and did little until individuals began pointing out what Nike was doing—and sometimes not even then.

For example, Bill Friday, the former president of the University of North Carolina (Michael Jordan's alma mater), blasted the university for letting Nike buy its way into Carolina's famous basketball program and hence into the larger university. "They [Nike] influence the coach's salary. They influence who wears what, and they prescribe what logo is worn," Friday observed. "I think they've gone too far."[35] Few in the state or federal governments, however, seemed to care if decisions in leading state schools were being purchased by private firms, as if the schools were simply up for auction. Critics of such auction sales nevertheless held to the belief that universities, after all, had interests and responsibilities quite different from those of private transnational companies.

Few cared about university sports departments being up for auction. After all, in other areas of American higher education university administrators and faculty sold themselves and their institutions to the highest bidder. Often, they felt they had little choice. State and federal monies to higher education were down. Alumni were unable or unwilling to make up for these cuts at many schools. Meanwhile those schools were being asked to educate increasing numbers of students in new as well as traditional fields of study. Some colleges saw little alternative but to sell themselves. In some instances, however, the auction resulted from simple greed, a kind of lust not lost on observing students. Some University of North Carolina students and faculty began organizing to stop some of the auctions.

They faced a steep uphill fight in challenging a firm that could stride over the world like the transnational colossus it had become. One type of 1996 Nike sneaker, for example, was designed in Oregon and Tennessee; cooperatively developed by technicians in Oregon, Taiwan, and South Korea; then manufactured in South Korea and Indonesia by putting together fifty-two separate components produced in five countries.[36] Every time someone laced up the sneaker, the wearer was being touched by a product in turn touched by people from at least a half-dozen nations.

Since the early 1990s, the media regularly reported that some of these people worked in subhuman conditions. To be sure, by the late 1990s, these conditions had improved too little. In Indonesian factories, where Nike made 70 million pairs of shoes in 1996, 25,000 workers each got $2.23 per day. Not a livable wage, critics charged. Low pay, however, formed only part of the problem. When Indonesians were forced to work as much as six hours a day overtime, and when they were beaten or sexually harassed by managers, the workers tried to form unions for self-protection. The mere threat of such unions brought in the military, which controlled Indonesia's government, to fire union organizers and maintain the status quo.[37]

Nike announced a code of conduct to protect workers. When a journalist interviewed a dozen workers, however, only one had even heard of the code. And it was obviously not being enforced. Some young Indonesians believed that if young Americans knew about these conditions and quit buying the sneakers, the situation would be corrected. One U.S. journalist, William Greider, said he did not even try to explain to Indonesians why American young people knew little, and cared less, about their problems—and that these Americans certainly would not quit buying sneakers for such reasons.

Working conditions in Vietnam were also terrible. Some twenty years after the United States had finally given up trying to destroy the Vietnamese Communist government in a savage war that lasted three decades (1945–1975), U.S. officials opened diplomatic relations with those same Communists in the mid-1990s. U.S., Japanese, and other transnationals rushed in to take advantage of cheap, disciplined labor. Indeed, the chance to exploit Vietnam's labor and emerging market was a central reason why relations with the former enemy had been established. In 1997, Thuyen Nguyen, of the U.S.-based Vietnam Labor Watch, visited the Nike plants. He reported that "Supervisors humiliate women, force them to kneel, to stand in the hot sun" for punishment, while paying them $1.60 for eight hours work. (It cost $2.00, observers estimated, to buy three meals a day in Vietnam.) More than 90 percent of the 35,000 workers were women who worked twelve-hour days to contribute the $2.00 labor cost for each pair of shoes. Workers reportedly fainted from exhaustion and malnutrition.[38]

Nike announced it had fired the manager of its main Vietnam factory. The company also joined with other transnationals in a media-covered meeting at the White House that set up a code of conduct for working conditions in the United States and abroad. Those signing included L. L. Bean, Reebok, Nike, and the television celebrity Kathie Lee Gifford. The code of conduct urged a sixty-hour maximum workweek and payment of legal minimum wages of the nations in which the plants were located. Critics declared the report weak. For example, they noted, minimum wages in some countries did not buy the food and shelter workers needed. The code's demand that workers be able to form unions was "pure hypocrisy," one critic announced, because the Asian nations (especially some militaries) refused to recognize union rights. President Bill Clinton and others at the signing ceremony nevertheless believed the code a beginning.[39]

Nike also tried to quiet the uproar by asking Andrew Young to investigate. Young, former ambassador to the United Nations, was a widely respected and politically powerful African-American politician. His report stated that Nike factories were "clean, organized, adequately ventilated and well lit," but labor rights needed more protection. He said he found no widespread or systematic abuse. Critics damned Young's report as "extremely shallow," based on quick visits to factories during which he depended on Nike-hired translators. The report, the critics continued, said far too little about the low wages.[40]

Phil Knight declared he would rapidly implement and improve upon Young's recommendations. Shortly thereafter, a Nike factory manager in Vietnam was sentenced to jail for physically abusing workers. Another manager fled Vietnam as he was being investigated for sexual abuse charges. Several months later, an internal Nike investigation became public. It concluded that a carcinogen, toluene, had been found in amounts even higher (some claimed 177 times higher) than Vietnamese law allowed. Toluene was known to damage the liver, kidneys, and central nervous system. Nike again announced it was moving quickly to remove this substance from its plants.[41]

In mid-1998, as the anti-Nike criticism was joined by a sharp drop in sneaker sales, Knight announced that the company would raise its minimum working age in Asian factories to eighteen, although current workers (some as young as fourteen) would not lose their jobs. At non-shoe factories, where toxic solvents and dangerous machinery were not used, the minimum age would be sixteen. Air quality controls were to be raised until they met U.S. standards. Knight said nothing about raising the one-dollar- or two-dollar-per-day wages of Indonesian and Chinese workers respectively. Critics applauded the improvements, but condemned Nike's refusal to pay "a living wage." They also insisted that the plants be closely monitored by independent agencies.[42]

The decline in Nike sneaker profits in 1997–1998 (they went down 49 percent from record sales of $9.6 billion) had little to do with labor conditions in its Asian factories. It had more to do with crashing Asian economies (especially Japan's), which created fierce competition and price-cutting. It also had something to do with an over-selling of the Swoosh. A number of buyers were simply tired of its presence everywhere they looked in the media. "There's a big backlash against Nike under way," one fashion analyst concluded. "The skateboard generation doesn't want to wear Nikes because their fathers wear them." Knight even decided to undertake a de-Swooshing campaign to make it less common. On some shoes the Swoosh was markedly inconspicuous. One line of Nikes, however, defied the sales downturn trend: Michael Jordan's brand increased in sales by 57 percent while every other major category of Nike footwear sold in the United States suffered steep falloffs. After Jordan scored the decisive basket in the final seconds of the 1998 NBA championship finals, his shoes "sailed out of stores," as one observer put it. Knight and Nike were holding tight to Jordan, almost as a life preserver, even as the star talked about retiring. Jordan and NBA basketball had helped make Nike a great transnational, and now—despite a fading Swoosh on the uniforms of no fewer than two hundred universities, and despite the endorsements of more than three thousand athletes worldwide—Nike, in its time of trials, depended increasingly on Jordan.[43]

## *Capital versus Culture:*
## *Implications and Conclusions*

Nike demonstrated how in the post-1970s world of the new transnational corporation, money was free to move anywhere it could find quick profit—but most people were not. The new capitalism, fueled by information age technology, had many sides, some well known to Americans, some unknown to (or ignored by) Americans.

In 1980, Michael Jordan, Phil Knight, Ted Turner, and Rupert Murdoch were not well known. Within little more than a decade, Jordan stood as the world's most popular sports and commercial figure; Knight's Nike dominated the sports product marketplace, which in turn dominated the world's public entertainment; while Murdoch and Turner, along with other transnationals such as Disney, Viacom, and Time-Warner (with whom Turner joined in 1996), shaped global media.

By the end of the 1990s, Murdoch's empire alone included 20th Century Fox Films, the *New York Post*, one-third ownership of the Golf television channel, the Fox television network, Fox Sports Brazil (a twenty-four-hour Portuguese-language cable channel), partnership with the ESPN sports network in Asia, part ownership of Fox Sports Australia, half ownership of the National Football League in Europe, and ties with other European and Asian (especially Chinese) media. To ensure that he had something to show on these many channels, Murdoch bought the Los Angeles Dodgers baseball team; the rights to televise major league baseball, football, and hockey; and part ownership of the New York Knicks basketball and Rangers hockey clubs. In mid-1998, Murdoch paid the most money ever shelled out for a sports franchise: $1 billion for the famous Manchester United soccer club. For many British, this was too much. Manchester United matches had always been shown to vast audiences on free or cable television, but Murdoch was clearly intending to display the team on his expensive pay-for-view television channels. He became Public Enemy No. 1 as British newspaper headlines screamed, MURDOCH MOST FOUL.[44]

Perhaps no one better caught the new era than the villain, Carver, in the 1997 James Bond film, *Tomorrow Never Dies.* Carver, in the eyes of many viewers, was based in part on Murdoch and his determination to control the globe's information systems. "Words are the new weapons," Carver proclaimed, and "satellites the new artillery. . . . Caesar had his legions, Napoleon had his armies, I have my divisions: TV, news, magazines—and by midnight tonight [when Carver believed he would control the entire China market], I'll reach more people than anyone save God himself."

"Carver" was only following out the logic of the new transnational capitalism born, with the help of revolutionary technology, in the 1970s and 1980s. Other giant media companies such as Cablevision, Comcast, and Disney also bought professional teams at high prices. Sports were not in the first place for fans, but for media which, like an out-of-control bacteria, always needed new material to stay alive twenty-four hours every day. The media then passed on the sport and its many commercial by-products to the fans—at a price.

James Naismith would not have been pleased. With his strong religious background and his immediate need to keep overactive young men busy during the winter months, he had hoped to develop human character through an interesting new sport. But his invention proved to be compatible with Knight's, Murdoch's, and Turner's ambitions a century later. Naismith's game quickly became valuable for the money it could generate. In a society based on business, and for a sport that from the start attracted large, loud audiences just at the point of century's turn when cities, transportation networks, and leisure time were booming, the commercialization was hardly surprising. With the advent of vast television audiences in the 1950s and 1960s, basketball's profitability leaped ahead.

David Stern, Michael Jordan, and Phil Knight built on these successes and, with the technology on which the revolutionary media was based, took the sport to marketplaces in all corners of the globe. As Stern summarized, when Jordan entered the league "the globalization of sports hadn't yet occurred. So the notion that someone would call me from Milan to say he watched [NBA basketball on] the German channel at 3 in the morning Sunday night because the Italian channel was tape-delaying it, although he got his results on CNN and nba.com, all those notions didn't exist in the '80s. And onto this exploding stage," Stern added, "walked a player of extraordinary talent and extraordinary personality, and almost defined the growth."[45]

Nike, the NBA, and Jordan grew rich together, but all paid a price for being dependent on the new media. Unlike other transnationals (for example, global oil companies such as Texaco or Chevron, which had long been able to keep their business dealings out of the public eye), Nike paraded its celebrity endorsers. But this made it a target, and as Nike sales and profits hit problems, the target was no longer as rapidly moving as it had been a decade earlier. Critics condemned the company's labor problems overseas. Some university officials—even Jordan's legendary coach at North Carolina, Dean Smith, who was otherwise revered for supporting good causes—tried to quiet the growing criticism of Nike. Despite such efforts, student groups sprang up at North Carolina, Michigan, Notre Dame, Illinois, and elsewhere (often emerging after class readings and discussions about the transnationals' problems) to focus attention on the sneaker industry's use of Asian labor and how American colleges and media had profited from such exploitation.[46]

One Nike endorser, Reggie White, star defensive end of the football champion Green Bay Packers, did speak out against the Asian and U.S. sweatshops. When White, however, also attacked homosexuality as unnatural and un-Christian, the ensuing uproar made the public forget his criticisms of Nike. Other endorsers, including golf champion Tiger Woods, tennis star Pete Sampras, and Jordan, remained silent. Jordan's repeated response was that he was "looking into it." Nike's direct and, to say the least, puzzling response to Reggie White's and others' criticisms came from a company spokesperson: "There are poor people everywhere. We need to pray for them all."[47]

A potentially more dangerous rebellion against Nike arose in a New York City public housing project. Leo Johnson, a director of youth activities, began a campaign to have his African-American youngsters return their sneakers to Nike because the company would not hire their unemployed parents to make shoes in the United States instead of Asia. Phil Knight refused to believe Johnson's pleas. Convinced that he and his youngsters "have the power to make these companies speak to [us] in more honest ways, not just show them Hollywood images of shirtless black men with their chests glistening with sweat," Johnson led a busload of his group to Nike's mid-Manhattan store. As columnist Harvey Araton recorded the event, "in the cold rain . . . , more sneakers were thrown back [at the store] like fish, while network cameras recorded the event for the evening news." The new media again carried the message. "We're at the bottom of the market," Johnson declared, "but if the bottom falls out" as inner-city youth refused to buy Nikes, "the whole thing can collapse." Michael Jordan was not recorded as having any comment.[48]

Unlike most athletes, sneaker executives, in their more direct moments, realized that they had run into a major problem in transnational capitalism. As a Reebok official observed, "We can't keep chasing wages around the globe forever like we do. There has to be a better way."[49]

The post-1970s commercial success of Jordan, Nike, the NBA, and Turner-Murdoch media raised other fundamental questions. Observers debated, for example, whether U.S.-based sports, media, and transnational corporations were parts of a new post-1960s imperialism that threatened to change (some would say corrupt), other cultures. After all, in 1998 all of Spain's ten most popular movies were American; in Great Britain, Germany, and Italy nine came from Hollywood; and even in France seven were U.S.-made. The U.S. dominance in film and television meant huge profits: in 1993, Americans made $4 billion more from Europeans than European film, television, and video sales earned from the Americans. By 1996 the gap shot up nearly 50 percent to almost $6 billion. U.S. influence, moreover, can be subtle. Where American television programs like *Blind Date* and *Wheel of Fortune* are not seen, other nations' copies of them are often highly popular. With its capital and technology, as one analyst observed, "America has written the 'grammar' of international television by creating its formats and concepts."[50]

Some analysts, such as former State Department official Joseph Nye, thought the United States would indeed wield its cultural power, and that everyone would benefit.

The soft power of the American media and popular culture would bestow on the world's peoples "its liberalism and egalitarian currents" by dominating "film, television and electronic communications." Soft power would make the twenty-first century "the period of America's greatest preeminence." Some examples of this "preeminence" were stunning. McDonald's, blaring Michael Jordan's endorsement, operated in 103 nations and fed one percent of the world's population each day. "Within the East Asian urban environment," one historian of the firm notes, "McDonald's fills a niche once occupied by the teahouse, the neighborhood shop, the street-side stall, and the park bench."[51]

Is such soft power a new information-age disguise for age-old imperialism? The reality is more complex, and interesting. *Webster's* defines imperialism as "the policy of extending the rule or authority of an empire or nation over foreign countries, or of acquiring and holding colonies and dependencies." Such a definition bears little relationship to the extension of transnational power since the 1970s. Certainly there was no interest in holding "colonies and dependencies" in the traditional political sense. And Europeans and Asians and Latin Americans did not have Nikes and Big Macs imposed on them against their will. Of special importance, the extension of that new power was not in the hands of states, but of corporations and individual capitalists such as Knight and Murdoch.

The Jordan-Knight-Murdoch-Turner phenomenon exemplified two central themes of the new information age and post–Cold-War era. One was an emphasis on acquiring vast, fresh markets (not an emphasis on military security)—markets best developed by huge amounts of capital. Another was the pivotal role played by transnationals and elite individuals (not nation-states or military alliances) in amassing the capital and creating the markets that quite willingly absorbed American popular culture once the media presented that culture.

Recent students of "post-imperialism" have taken these themes a step farther. They argue that transnational corporations have created in many nations a new class—a native "nationalist managerial" class—which works to help the transnational spread its power among people of whom this new class is a part. Thus it is in the interest of cable and television companies in Europe, or shoe stores in Latin America, to sell Murdoch's or Knight's products because they can fetch a good price from customers who admire Michael Jordan. This post-1970s class can provide a vital support on the important local political level for transnationals. The new corporations thus not only change buying habits in a society, but modify the composition of the society itself. For the society that receives it, soft power can have hard effects.[52]

Do these transnationals/new media embody a more specific cultural imperialism? For example, does U.S. culture and its ideology exert imperialist control over other cultures and alter their ideology? This has been intensely debated since the information age began in the 1960s and 1970s. Cultural imperialism is a new term dating probably from the 1960s. Analysts cannot agree on exactly what it is or how it works. Indeed, there is little consensus on what "culture" is, other than a vague "way of life" in a given society.[53]

Todd Gitlin, an analyst of culture and sociology, commented on the debate: "[W]hile the culture warriors have been revising books, cultural conservatives," Gitlin observed, "have been revising global markets to their benefit." Gitlin demanded that the debate center on politics and economics: "Conceivably, someday, a critical mass of student activists will learn how to spark movements that address poverty, environmental degradation, and war."[54]

Those who "have been revising global markets," to use Gitlin's phrase, understand how politics and economics drive culture. Public figures who represent the transnationals, such as Michael Jordan, might try to move above politics and refuse to take positions on such thorny issues as exploited Asian labor. But transnationals cannot, in reality, be neutral on such issues. They have to take political positions because the politics and economic benefits (or losses) are interrelated. When faced with the imperative to take political positions, they have responded in one of three ways: they back down in order to save their market, they use their leverage to force a political critic to back down, or they (usually with great reluctance) appeal to a government to help them protect their market.

An example of the first—backing down in order to save the market—occurred when Murdoch changed his news programs, especially regarding Hong Kong, so as to avoid a Communist Chinese government blockade of his television network. In 1998, Murdoch again surrendered to the Chinese. Chris Patten, Hong Kong's last British Governor, wrote a book highly critical of the Communist officials' attempt to humiliate him and other British officials, while China reneged on some agreements. Patten's book was to be published by Murdoch's HarperCollins publishing house in London. But when the Chinese attacked the book's contents, Murdoch and HarperCollins cancelled its publication. Critics charged that HarperCollins surrendered because Murdoch's Star TV satellite channel, based in Hong Kong, wanted to dominate the vast Chinese market. Patten's book received wide attention when published by Macmillan, but as one HarperCollins author, novelist Doris Lessing, observed of Murdoch's decision:

"It is so shocking I can't find words for it." In London, HarperCollins's editor-in-chief, Stuart Profitt, resigned over Murdoch's decision.[55]

An example of the second type of political action—using their leverage to force critics to back down—was exemplified when an independent filmmaker made a documentary about Nike's contract factories in Southeast Asia. CBS was interested in the film, but then refused to show it. Critics charged that CBS's decision was directly related to the network accepting large amounts of advertising from Nike. At the Olympics, CBS commentators even wore jackets decorated by the Swoosh while on camera, a form of advertising that received blistering attacks from viewers who saw the jackets as a CBS sellout of its objectivity where Nike, or athletes who endorsed Nike goods, might be involved.[56]

The third type of political action—appealing to the government for help—occurred at a White House ceremony. On this occasion, the President of the United States and Phil Knight jointly approved the agreement to treat Southeast Asian laborers better.

"Soft power," it seems, can become a mere cover for "tough power"—that is, the tough creation of important new classes, and the tough politics of transnational-government relations. The larger question is whether this combination of soft and tough power will, in Nye's words, make the twenty-first century "the period of America's greatest preeminence."

One important dissent from Nye's thesis came from Samuel Huntington, whose *Clash of Civilizations and the Remaking of World Order* (1996) was widely debated. Huntington suggested that cultures, especially religious-based cultures, such as Islam, Hinduism, and Confucianism as well as Christianity, would conflict, and that this conflict would to a great degree shape twenty-first-century global affairs. Huntington argued that some of these cultures already viewed U.S. culture as a dangerous, corrupting influence that had to be stopped, if necessary, by force.

Huntington's thesis seemed to turn into reality in mid-1998 when bombs blew up U.S. diplomatic embassies in Kenya and Tanzania. Twelve Americans and more than 250 Africans died. The U.S. government blamed the blasts on Osama bin Laden, an Islamic fundamentalist. Bin Laden hated the United States for, in his view, corrupting his native Saudi Arabia through the stationing of U.S. troops and the growing influence of American culture in that country. The United States struck back with missile attacks on bin Laden's supposed supply bases in Afghanistan and Sudan. U.S. officials declared what they termed a "new war"—the "war of the future"—against terrorists such as bin Laden.[57]

Clearly, the expansion of transnationals and American culture was not universally hailed. But equally clearly, the opposition—contrary to Huntington—did not run only along the lines of different "civilizations," as he termed them. When French leaders, German newspapers, and Canadian observers condemned the inroads of American influence, the condemnation came from within the "civilization" that included the United States. Indeed, some analysts suggested that most critical splits in our new information age would occur between moderates and political radicals (or religious fundamentalists) *within* each "civilization."[58] In the United States, the worst terrorist attacks of the 1990s (such as the bombing of the Oklahoma City Federal Building that killed 168 people), were the work of few U.S. citizens who saw the U.S. government as engaged in a vast conspiracy against individuals' freedom. Bin Laden himself had been thrown out of Saudi Arabia by Saudi conservatives.

In the post-1970s information age, neither the "clash of civilizations" nor the clash of capital with a culture could be easily and simply described. But some tried. Two authors who celebrated American triumphialism in the aftermath of the Cold War wrote in 1997 that "the end of the Cold War also saw the triumph of a set of ideas long championed by the United States: those of the free-market economy and to some extent [*sic*] liberal democracy. . . . This cleared the way," they believed, "for the creation of a truly global economy. . . . Everybody on the planet [is] in the same economy."[59] But as people as different as the French Cultural Minister and Osama bin Laden illustrated, not "everybody" wanted to be in that "same economy" if American principles and images were to dominate it. By late 1998, moreover, that "truly global economy" was in deep trouble. Many nations, led by Malaysia, Russia, and the new Chinese territory of Hong Kong (once a rabid free-market bastion), began to rebel against the U.S. "free-market economy and . . . liberal democracy." They did so for two reasons: First, they had developed doubts about that economy and democracy. And second, they turned against U.S. leadership after concluding that the power of transnationals, especially banks, had become dangerous to their economic survival, and even corrupt.

These recent crises highlighted an interesting and explosive paradox noted by Huntington. Millions of Americans now make their living in the world economy, either at home or abroad. These Americans, however, remain alien to—even quite ignorant of—the cultures that pay their bills. Consequently when other peoples react, sometimes with violence, against U.S. influence, Americans tend to turn inward, or respond unilaterally and angrily. Both of those responses—turning inward or responding unilaterally (and sometimes with force)—are deeply rooted in the American character. The roots go back, indeed, several centuries and are accurately called "isolationism." These two responses in our time are deeply problematic, for in the integrated electronic global village, turning inward is impossible and unilaterally using force in such a village can be suicidal.

To understand this new age and avoid self-destruction, we must understand the transnationals such as Nike and the media empires of Murdoch and Turner that are based on revolutionary technology. The long commercial history of basketball's evolution in the marketplace, and the career of Michael Jordan as a culmination of that evolution, help us in this.

The battlefields ahead, then, will revolve not around imperialism versus anti-imperialism, or civilization versus civilization, but capital versus culture. The Cold War between American capitalism and Russian Communism dominated much of the twentieth century. At the end of that day, the West had adjusted to the post-1970s technology and Communism had not. America and capitalism stood triumphant. After 1991, the nature of the struggle noticeably changed. It was now between new, technological forms of capitalism versus cultures pressured to adjust to changes demanded by the capital. As the *Economist* phrased it with slight exaggeration, the "1,000 . . . people who run the world" do "not mind whether an idea, a technique or a market is (in Mr. Huntington's complex scheme) Sinic, Hindu, Islamic or Orthodox. If an idea works or a market arises," these thousand people "will grab it."[60]

Capital will ultimately win this new contest, just as it has broken down political, economic, social, and geographical barriers since its appearance in a recognizable modern form five hundred years ago. At the end of the millennium, as Masao Miyoshi observed, the new transnational capitalism "converts most social and political issues into economy, and culture into a commercial program. Arts and architecture are absorbed into business." Sports can be added to that list. Unless controlled, this contest between capital and culture will not be orderly and peaceful. It is an irony that Americans love order and seek stability, but insist on expanding a capitalism that often undermines order and generates violent instability. This is precisely what occurred during the first great wave of U.S. corporate expansionism abroad after the 1880s, and on a much larger scale it is occurring a century later. *New York Times* columnist Thomas Friedman argued that many nations, including such friends as the French and Japanese, believed the United States is "the capital of global arrogance." The reasons for this feeling, he added, were U.S. economic successes and how Americans sometimes "throw their weight around unfairly." "And part of it is because Americanization, from Mickey Mouse to Microsoft, has become a powerful, tempting and frequently destabilizing force, challenging every traditional society."[61]

In the late 1990s, some nations began to discuss how to control that struggle to prevent U.S. influences and the disruption those influences have generated. As noted above, a few nations, led by Malaysia and Hong Kong, placed some controls on foreign capital. A mid-1998 conference called by the Canadian government convened nineteen nations, but did not include the United States. The conference discussed how to keep U.S. cultural influences out while nurturing ordinary commerce. The United Nations sponsored a similar meeting in Sweden. European officials met in England to discuss "the Digital Age," but as the *Economist* noted, the real subject was "How Can We Keep the Americans, Especially Rupert Murdoch, Out?" Murdoch actually appeared at the conference. His message was direct: "eliminate barriers to the free flow of capital, labor, and talent."[62] The other conference delegates held a different view. To them, since labor did not move easily, and since capital could control talent, the real problem was capital—such as Murdoch's.

James Naismith, the commercial development of basketball, post-1970s technology, and the transnational corporation transformed how many Americans spent their time in the late twentieth century. Michael Jordan, Phil Knight, Rupert Murdoch, and Ted Turner—all linked together in the global marketplace—also transformed how much of the rest of the world spent its time as the new millennium approached. Whether all this will be for the long-term benefit of the world's peoples remained a central question. Multibillionaire George Soros, one of the more thoughtful global capitalists, warned that "We can have a market economy, but we cannot have a market society."[63] Americans had hardly begun in the 1990s to think through that distinction, even though it was the problem posed by Nike, Murdoch, and Michael Jordan-endorsed products, which made little distinction between market economies and market societies.

In the new tightly wired world, Americans cannot escape these questions. They can only begin to deal with them by understanding the history of how we all became part of a global market economy and market society.

# Acknowledgments

This book began when a long-time friend, Alan Kraut of American University, asked for a contribution to a series of American biographies that might be used in classrooms. His encouragement, patience, and friendship lasted through a number of major changes in topic, approach, and publisher, and for all that I am most indebted to him. Sherman Cochran, Martin Sklar, Evan Stewart, Dan Weil, Dick and Jo Hershberger, Ambassador Eric Edelman, Jim Siekmeier, and Geoff Smith sent helpful materials, which were nearly as appreciated as their long friendships. A large debt is owed to Parviz Parvizi for his invaluable research help and to Stephen Weiss for his friendship and support. Max Perelman kindly allowed the use of his unpublished account about encountering Michael Jordan's fame in a remote Chinese village. Ed Barber, Vice President of W. W. Norton, has again been a valued friend and editor, not least because most of his ideas about basketball and capitalism agree with mine. I am indebted to Margaret Farley for superb copyediting. The book benefited from conversations over the years about sports with many friends, especially Joel Silbey,

David Maisel, Richard Cutler, Gerry McCauley (who also again offered wise advice about placing this manuscript), Arthur Kaminsky, David Langbart, Larry Malley, Michael Kammen, Mary Beth Norton, Larry Moore, Walter Nugent, Lloyd Gardner, Tom McCormick, and, of course, Scott LaFeber, Suzanne and Tom Kahl, Bill and Hilde Kahl, and—more involuntarily but with more excitement—Sandy LaFeber. The book is dedicated to two young men who will write their own accounts in the sports and media of the twenty-first century.

# Notes

## Preface

1. A useful introduction to, and discussion of, many of these terms is Joyce Appleby et al., *Knowledge and Postmodernism in Historical Perspective* (New York, 1996); see also Fredric Jameson and Masao Miyoshi, eds., *The Cultures of Globalization* (Durham, N.C., 1998). In the Preface, Jameson writes: "Globalization—even the term itself has been hotly contested—is thus the modern or postmodern version of the proverbial elephant, described by its blind observers in so many diverse ways. Yet one can still posit the existence of the elephant in the absence of a single persuasive and dominant theory. . . ." Jameson adds that "the concept of globalization reflects the sense of an immense enlargement of world communication, as well as of the horizon of a world market. . . . Roland Robertson . . . has formulated the dynamics of globalization as 'the twofold process of the particularization of the universal and the universalization of the particular.'" Jameson agrees, but emphasizes, as does *Michael Jordan and the New Global Capitalism,* the "antagonism and tension between these two poles" (pp. xi–xii). In *Michael Jordan . . . ,* "globalization" is used to describe the spread of transnationals and technology across the globe, while "Americanization" is the U.S. domination of this process.

2. *Time,* June 17, 1996, p. 79.

3. *Sports Illustrated,* Dec. 8, 1997, p. 33.

4. *Economist,* Sept. 6, 1997, p. 22.

5. Definitions of "culture" are many and varied. One working definition is Daniel Bell's: "Culture here are the binding fidelities of consciousness, rooted in history and tradition, kinship and race, religion and nationality, that shape the emotional consanguinity, literal or fictive, among individuals and make them one." Daniel Bell, *The Cultural Contradictions of Capitalism* (New York, 1996), p. 332. Historic changes in the decentralization of the transmission of popular culture are interestingly traced in Greg MacDonald, *The Emergence of Global Multi-Media Conglomerates* (Geneva, 1990), esp. pp. 1–2.

6. John Cassidy, "The Next Thinker: The Return of Karl Marx," *New Yorker,* Oct. 20–27, 1997, p. 251; Allen Guttmann, *Games and Empires: Modern Sports and Cultural Imperialism* (New York, 1994), pp. 31–32.

7. Geoffrey S. Smith, "The Roar of the Greasepaint, the Smell of the Crowd?" *Queen's Quarterly,* 103 (Fall 1996), pp. 3–19.

8. *Washington Post,* Sept. 25, 1997, p. A25.

9. *Ibid.,* Nov. 4, 1997, p. A1.

10. The widening debate over the power of American culture can be glimpsed in Roland Robertson, "Mapping the Global Condition: Globalization as the Central Concept," *Theory, Culture, and Society,* 7 (June 1990), pp. 15–30; Frederick Buell, *National Culture and the New Global System* (Baltimore, 1994), esp. pp. 4–5, 9; Anthony D. Smith, "Towards a Global Culture," *Theory, Culture, and Society,* 7 (June 1990), esp. p. 180; Peter L. Berger, "Four Faces of Global Culture," *National Interest,* no. 49 (Fall 1997), pp. 23–29.

11. Nicholas D. Kristof column in *New York Times,* Feb. 1, 1998, p. 1; *New York Times,* Feb. 13, 1998, p. D1; *Economist,* July 25, 1998, pp. 28.

12. Henry Kissinger, "Perils of Globalism," *Washington Post,* Oct. 5, 1998, p. A21.

13. *Chicago Tribune,* Jan. 12 and 14, 1999.

14. *Ibid.,* Jan. 13, 1999, sec. 3, pp. 1, 4; *Washington Post,* Jan. 14, 1999, p. A8; *Washington Post,* Jan. 13, 1999, p. D4.

## Chapter One

1. *Washington Post,* Aug. 18, 1993, p. A20.
2. Phil Jackson and Hugh Delehanty, *Sacred Hoops* (New York, 1995), p. 17.
3. Mike Lupica, "Let's Fly Again," *Esquire,* 123 (May 1995), p. 54; John Hoberman, *Darwin's Athletes* (Boston, 1997), p. 9.
4. Jim Naughton, *Taking to the Air: The Rise of Michael Jordan* (New York, 1992), pp. 39–40.
5. *Ibid.*
6. *Ibid.,* p. 42.
7. Bob Greene, *Hang Time* (New York, 1992), p. 44.
8. John Feinstein, "A Coach's Composure . . . ," *Washington Post,* March 30, 1982, sec. D, p. 4.
9. Arthur Ashe, Jr., *A Hard Road to Glory: A History of the African-American Athlete,* 3 vols. (New York, 1988), III, p. 79.
10. Jackson and Delehanty, *Sacred Hoops,* p. 174.
11. Naughton, *Taking to the Air,* pp. 60–62.
12. *Chicago Tribune,* June 20, 1984, sec. 4, p. 1.
13. *New York Times,* May 29, 1994, p. S11.
14. Keith Myerscough, "The Game with No Name: The Invention of Basketball," *International Journal of the History of Sport,* XII (April 1995), pp. 148–151.
15. *Ibid.,* p. 148.
16. Douglas A. Noverr and Lawrence E. Ziewacz, *The Games They Played: Sports in American History, 1865–1980* (Chicago, 1983), p. 32.
17. Stephen H. Hardy, "Entrepreneurs, Organizations, and the Sports Marketplace," in S. W. Pope, ed., *The New American Sport History* (Urbana and Chicago, 1997), pp. 356–357; Elliott Gorn, "Sports Through the Nineteenth Century," in *ibid.,* p. 54; Peter Levine, *A. G. Spalding and the Rise of Baseball* (New York, 1985), which has useful references to basketball, too.
18. Steven A. Riess, *City Games* (Urbana, Ill., 1989), pp. 107–108, 117; Ted Vincent, *Mudville's Revenge: The Rise and Fall of American Sport* (Lincoln, Neb., 1981), pp. 225–226.
19. Vincent, *Mudville's Revenge,* p. 233; Naughton, *Taking to the Air,* p. 140.

20. Allen Guttmann, *The Erotic in Sports* (New York, 1996), p. 79.
21. Riess, *City Games*, pp. 108, 117.
22. Ashe, *Hard Road to Glory*, II, pp. 47–50; *New York Times*, March 9, 1997, p. S8; Naughton, *Taking to the Air*, p. 141.
23. Ashe, *Hard Road to Glory*, III, 50–51.
24. Vincent, *Mudville's Revenge*, p. 314.
25. Ashe, *Hard Road to Glory*, III, p. 72; Jeff Jansen, "Jordan Still King," *Advertising Age*, April 25, 1994, p. 59.
26. Noverr and Ziewacz, *Games They Played*, pp. 333–337; Ashe, *Hard Road to Glory*, III, p. 74.
27. Lawrence M. Kahn and Peter D. Sherer, "Racial Discrimination in the National Basketball Association," in Paul D. Staudohar and James A. Mangan, eds., *The Business of Professional Sports* (Urbana, Ill., 1991), p. 72.
28. David K. Wiggins, " 'Great Speed but Little Stamina': The Historical Debate Over Black Athletic Superiority," in S. W. Pope, ed., *The New American Sport History* (Urbana and Chicago, 1997), pp. 320–324.
29. Ashe, *Hard Road to Glory*, III, p. 79; Naughton, *Taking to the Air*, p. 94.

## Chapter Two

1. Allen Guttmann, "Mediated Spectatorship," in S. W. Pope, ed., *The New American Sport History* (Urbana and Chicago, 1997), p. 379.
2. Bob Greene, *Hang Time* (Chicago, 1992), p. 61.
3. *Current Biography*, 58 (Feb. 1997), p. 25.
4. Jim Naughton, *Taking to the Air* (New York, 1992), p. 28.
5. Robert Lipsyte and Peter Levine, *Idols of the Game: A Sporting History of the American Century* (Atlanta, Ga., 1995), p. 330.
6. Naughton, *Taking to the Air*, pp. 121–128.
7. Phil Jackson and Hugh Delehanty, *Sacred Hoops* (New York, 1995), pp. 80–81.
8. *Sports Illustrated*, June 23, 1997, p. 34.
9. Jackson and Delehanty, *Sacred Hoops*, pp. 4, 80.
10. Naughton, *Taking to the Air*, p. 150.

11. *New York Times,* June 7, 1997, p. 31.
12. This section on the new transnationals' characteristics draws especially from Robert G. Hawkins and Ingo Walter, "Multinational Corporations. . . ." in U.S. Congress, Joint Economic Committee, *Special Study on Economic Change, Volume 9* (Washington, D.C., 1980), pp. 703–704, 723; Richard J. Barnet and John Cavanagh, *Global Dreams* (New York, 1994), pp. 15, 168–173; John H. Dunning, *Globalization* (Dublin, Ireland, 1993), pp. 4–6, 31; William Greider, *One World, Ready or Not* (New York, 1997), esp. pp. 21–22; Peter Dicken, "Transnational Corporations and Nation-States," *International Social Science Review,* 49 (March 1997), esp. pp. 77–78.
13. Milton Moskowitz, "Rebel with a Cause," *Business and Society Review,* no. 94 (Summer 1995), p. 66, which also reviews and quotes from Donald Katz's excellent, *Just Do It: The Nike Spirit in the Corporate World* (New York, 1994).
14. Katz, *Just Do It,* p. 66.
15. Frank Deford, "Running Man," *Vanity Fair,* 56 (August 1993), p. 52.
16. Naughton, *Taking to the Air,* p. 6.
17. Katz, *Just Do It,* p. 66.
18. *Ibid.,* pp. 200–201.
19. *Ibid.,* pp. 136–137.
20. Randall Rothenberg, *Where the Suckers Moon* (New York, 1994), p. 203.
21. *Ibid.,* pp. 214–215.
22. Geraldine E. Willigan, "High-Performance Marketing: An Interview with Nike's Phil Knight," *Harvard Business Review,* 70 (July 1992), p. 96.
23. Naughton, *Taking to the Air,* p. 151.
24. *Ibid.,* p. 91.
25. Dori Jones Yang, "How Nike Blasted Off," *Business Week,* April 6, 1992, p. 10.
26. John Hoberman, *Darwin's Athletes* (Boston, 1997), p. 34.
27. Jeff Coplon, "Legends, Champions?" *New York Times Magazine,* April 21, 1996, p. 35.
28. Hoberman, *Darwin's Athletes,* p. 34.
29. Katz, *Just Do It,* p. 148.

30. *Ibid.,* p. 243.
31. *Ibid.,* p. 28.
32. Richard L. Sklar, *Postimperialism: Concepts and Implications* (Hanover, N.H., 1997), p. 16.
33. Marcy Magiera, "Nike Takes Global Steps," *Advertising Age,* Aug. 1, 1994, p. 34.
34. *Advertising Age,* Aug. 1, 1994, p. 34.
35. Katz, *Just Do It,* p. 86; Naughton, *Taking to the Air,* p. 5.
36. Hamid Mowlana, *Global Information and World Communication* (New York, 1986), pp. 85–86; Barnet and Cavanagh, *Global Dreams,* pp. 168–173.
37. Guttmann, "Mediated Spectatorship," p. 372.
38. Mowlana, *Global Information,* p. 70.
39. Greg MacDonald, *The Emergence of Global Multi-Media Conglomerates* (Geneva, 1990), p. 22.
40. Wilson Dizard, Jr., *Old Media/New Media: Mass Communications in the Information Age* (New York, 1994), p. 42.
41. *Ibid.,* p. 3.
42. Mowlana, *Global Information,* pp. 82–85.
43. Robert Goldberg and Gerald Jay Goldberg, *Citizen Turner* (New York, 1995) is a colorful, detailed biography; Turner is also analyzed in Ken Auletta, *The Highwaymen: Warriors of the Information Superhighway* (New York, 1997), esp. pp. 207–211.
44. Robert L. Stevenson, "Cable News Network," in Bruce Jentleson and Thomas Paterson, eds., *Encyclopedia of U.S. Foreign Relations,* 4 vols. (New York, 1997), II, p. 207.
45. Auletta, *The Highwaymen,* p. 260; a good, brief analysis of Murdoch's career from a former insider is Andrew Weil, "Murdoch and Me," *Vanity Fair,* 25 (Dec. 1996), pp. 180–206.
46. *Variety,* May 27, 1991, pp. 35, 37.

## Chapter Three

1. *Time,* Jan. 9, 1989, pp. 50–52.
2. Jerome Holtzman, "Jordan Finds Teammates," *Chicago Tribune,* June 11, 1991, sec. 4, p. 1.
3. Roger G. Noll, "Professional Basketball: Economic and Business Perspectives," in Paul D. Staudohar and James A. Man-

gan, eds., *The Business of Professional Sports* (Urbana, Ill., 1991), p. 33.

4. *Ebony,* 47 (Nov. 1991), pp. 72–74.

5. *Chicago Tribune,* June 17, 1991, sec. 7, p. 3, conveniently ran the highlights of the 1990–1991 season.

6. Paul Sullivan, "747 . . . ," *Chicago Tribune,* June 17, 1991, sec. 7, p. 5.

7. *Chicago Tribune,* June 13, 1991, sec. 4, pp. 1, 5.

8. Jim Naughton, *Taking to the Air: The Rise of Michael Jordan* (New York, 1992), pp. 10–11.

9. *Time,* June 24, 1991, p. 46.

10. Paul Sullivan, "Living Legend . . . ," *Chicago Tribune,* June 13, 1991, sec. 4, p. 1.

11. *Sports Illustrated,* Dec. 23, 1991, pp. 65–66.

12. Naughton, *Taking to the Air,* p. 149.

13. *Los Angeles Times,* June 1, 1991, p. D1.

14. Ira Berkow, "Air Jordan . . . ," *New York Times,* June 15, 1991, sec. 1, p. 29.

15. *Chicago Tribune,* June 2, 1991, sec. 1, pp. 1, 18.

16. Nicola and Marino de Medici, "Foreign Intervention: Europe Invades America," *Public Opinion,* 9 (Feb.–March 1986), pp. 17–20.

17. Frank Costigliola, *Awkward Dominion: American Political, Economic, and Cultural Relations with Europe, 1919–1933* (Ithaca, N.Y., 1984), pp. 19–20, 175–176.

18. Richard Grenier, "Around the World in American Ways," *Public Opinion,* 9 (Feb.–March 1986), p. 58.

19. Jack McCallum quoted in *Current Biography,* 58 (Feb. 1997), p. 24.

20. Geraldine E. Willigan, "High-Performance Marketing: An Interview with Nike's Phil Knight," *Harvard Business Review,* 70 (July 1992), p. 99.

21. *Ibid.,* pp. 96–98.

22. Donald Katz, *Just Do It: The Nike Spirit in the Corporate World* (New York, 1994), p. 41.

23. Mark Vancil, ed., *The NBA at Fifty* (New York, 1996), p. 239.

24. Naughton, *Taking to the Air,* pp. 3, 15.

25. Mike Lupica, "Let's Fly Again," *Esquire,* 123 (May 1995), p. 52.

26. Bob Greene, *Hang Time* (New York, 1992), p. 286.
27. Phil Jackson and Hugh Delehanty, *Sacred Hoops* (New York, 1995), p. 157; *Chicago Tribune,* March 21, 1992, sec. 3, p. 1.
28. Jack McCallum, "Everywhere Man," *Sports Illustrated,* Dec. 23, 1991, p. 69.

## Chapter Four

1. Rick Telander, "Senseless," *Sports Illustrated,* May 14, 1990, pp. 37–38.
2. *Ibid.,* p. 38.
3. John Hoberman, *Darwin's Athletes* (Boston, 1997), p. 264 footnote.
4. Bob Greene, *Hang Time* (New York, 1992), p. 208; Telander, "Senseless," p. 49.
5. Jim Naughton, *Taking to the Air: The Rise of Michael Jordan* (New York, 1992), p. 136; Merrill J. Melnick and Donald Sabo, "Sport and Social Mobility among African-American and Hispanic Athletes," in George Eisen and David K. Wiggins, eds., *Ethnicity and Sport in North American History and Culture* (Westport, Conn., 1994), pp. 230–231.
6. Melnick and Sabo, "Sport and Social Mobility among African-American and Hispanic Athletes," p. 231.
7. Naughton, *Taking to the Air,* pp. 215–216.
8. Hoberman, *Darwin's Athletes,* pp. 31–32.
9. *Advertising Age,* Oct. 29, 1990, p. 59.
10. Curry Kirkpatrick, "The Unlikeliest Homeboy," *Sports Illustrated,* Dec. 23, 1991, pp. 72, 75.
11. Lynn Norment, "Michael and Juanita Jordan," *Ebony,* 47 (Nov. 1991), p. 75.
12. *Chicago Tribune,* March 29, 1992, sec. 1, p. 1.
13. *Ibid.,* March 21, 1992, sec. 3, p. 1.
14. *New York Times,* March 27, 1992, sec. B, p. 10.
15. *Chicago Tribune,* April 1, 1992, sec. 4, p. 1; *ibid.,* April 2, 1992, sec. 1, p. 22.
16. *New York Times,* Aug. 2, 1992, sec. 8, p. 1.
17. *Ibid.*
18. *Boston Globe,* Aug. 2, 1992, p. 47.
19. *New York Post,* July 30, 1992, p. 64.

20. *Boston Globe,* Aug. 2, 1997, p. 52; *ibid.,* Aug. 9, 1997, p. 52.

21. The Reuters Library report, Aug. 9, 1992.

22. *Newsweek* quoting John Horan, May 20, 1996, p. 60.

23. Donald Katz, *Just Do It: The Nike Spirit in the Corporate World* (New York, 1994), p. 25; Dan Weil, "Pro Athlete Endorsements . . . ," Bloomberg L. P. wire story, Dec. 15, 1997.

24. Anne Swardson and Sandra Bugawara, "Asian Workers Become Customers," *Washington Post,* Dec. 30, 1996, pp. A1, A16.

25. *Washington Post,* Dec. 30, 1996, p. A16.

26. *Far Eastern Economic Review,* Nov. 5, 1992, pp. 58–59.

27. Geraldine E. Willigan, "High Performance Marketing: An Interview with Nike's Phil Knight," *Harvard Business Review,* 70 (July 1992), p. 92.

28. *Far Eastern Economic Review,* Nov. 5, 1992, p. 60.

29. *Ibid.*

30. Henny Sender, "Sprinting to the Forefront," *Far Eastern Economic Review,* Aug. 1, 1996, pp. 50–51; Katz, *Just Do It,* esp. pp. 177–179.

31. Richard J. Barnet and John Cavanagh, *Global Dreams: Imperial Corporations and the New World Order* (New York, 1994), pp. 326–328.

32. *Washington Post,* Dec. 30, 1996, p. A16.

33. *Public Relations Journal,* 49 (July 1993), p. 4.

34. Katz, *Just Do It,* pp. 195–196.

35. *Ibid.,* p. 198.

36. *Brandweek,* Dec. 7, 1992, p. 4; *Adweek's Marketing Week,* 33 (June 1992), pp. 1, 6.

37. *Wall Street Journal,* July 22, 1993, p. A1.

38. A leading work on "soft power" is Joseph Nye, Jr., *Bound to Lead* (New York, 1990).

39. Richard Pells, *Not Like Us* (New York, 1997), pp. 241–242.

40. *Ibid.,* pp. 233, 267, 300–301.

41. Nathan Gardels, "The Higher the Satellite . . . ," *New Perspectives Quarterly,* 8 (Fall 1991), pp. 42–44; Flora Lewis column in *New York Times,* Sept. 17, 1982, sec. A, p. 23.

42. Ken Auletta, *The Highwaymen: Warriors of the Information Superhighway* (New York, 1997), pp. 266–268.

## Chapter Five

1. *Chicago Tribune,* Oct. 23, 1992, sec. 4, p. 1.
2. Dave Anderson, "Jordan's Atlantic City Caper," *New York Times,* May 27, 1993, sec. B, p. 11; *Chicago Tribune,* May 28, 1993, sec. 4, p. 1 has Jackson quote.
3. *Chicago Tribune,* May 28, 1993, sec. 4, p. 7.
4. William C. Rhoden, "The Issue Is Bigger than Jordan," *New York Times,* June 5, 1992, sec. 1, p. 29.
5. *Advertising Age,* June 7, 1993, p. 2.
6. *New York Times,* June 5, 1993, sec. 1, p. 29.
7. *Chicago Tribune,* June 9, 1993, sec. 1, p. 3.
8. *Ibid.,* June 22, 1993, sec. 3, p. 4.
9. *New York Post,* June 21, 1993, p. 47.
10. *Chicago Tribune,* June 6, 1993, sec. 1, p. 1; *ibid,* June 21, 1993, sec. 3, p. 7.
11. *Ibid.,* July 7, 1993, sec. 1, p. 1.
12. *New York Times,* Aug. 16, 1993, sec. C, p. 1.
13. Donald Katz, *Just Do It: The Nike Spirit in the Corporate World* (New York, 1994), p. 279.
14. Robert Lipsyte and Peter Levine, *Idols of the Game: A Sporting History of the American Century* (Atlanta, Ga., 1995), p. 334.
15. Bob Greene, *Rebound: The Odyssey of Michael Jordan* (New York, 1995), pp. 3–4.
16. *Ibid.,* pp. 54–55.
17. *Advertising Age,* Oct. 11, 1993, p. 48.
18. Jeff Jensen, "Nike, Gatorade . . . ," *ibid.,* March 21, 1994, pp. 4, 42; Jeff Jensen, "Jordan Basketball Era Inspires New Products," *ibid.,* Dec. 12, 1994, p. 30.
19. Jeff Coplon, "Legends, Champions?" *New York Times Magazine,* April 21, 1996, p. 37.
20. Tom Verducci, "Keeping His Guard Up," *Sports Illustrated,* Dec. 12, 1994, pp. 94–97.
21. Christy Fisher, " 'Made in USA' Tells Nike: Come Home," *Advertising Age,* Oct. 26, 1992, pp. 3, 49.
22. *Business Week,* April 18, 1994, p. 87.
23. Phil Jackson and Huge Delehanty, *Sacred Hoops* (New York, 1995), p. 20.

24. Alexander Wolff, "55," *Sports Illustrated,* Nov. 13, 1995, pp. 108–121.
25. Jackson and Delehanty, *Sacred Hoops,* pp. 196–198.

## *Chapter Six*

1. *Current Biography,* 58 (Feb. 1997), p. 26.
2. *New York Times,* May 25, 1996, sec. 8, p. 2.
3. John Hoberman, *Darwin's Athletes* (Boston, 1997), p. 42; *New York Times,* May 23, 1996, sec. 8, p. 2.
4. *Chicago Tribune,* June 16, 1996, sec. 8, p. 3.
5. *Ibid.,* June 17, 1996, sec. 3, p. 4.
6. *Sports Illustrated,* June 30, 1997, p. 14.
7. Harvey Araton, "Jordan's Magnificent Desperation," *New York Times,* June 9, 1996, sec. 8, p. 1.
8. *New York Times,* May 16, 1997, p. B10.
9. *Newsweek,* June 29, 1998, p. 59.
10. Bob Greene, *Hang Time: Days and Dreams with Michael Jordan* (New York, 1992), p. 358.
11. Mike Lupica, "Amazing Grace," *Esquire,* 123 (Feb. 1995), p. 62.
12. *Chicago Tribune,* April 25, 1996, sec. 7, p. 18; *USA Today,* Dec. 12, 1997, p. 18C.
13. *Washington Post,* June 26, 1997, p. D8; *Time,* Sept. 22, 1997, p. 22.
14. *Business Week,* April 7, 1997, p. 44.
15. Jeff Coplon, "Legends. Champions?" *New York Times Magazine,* April 21, 1996, p. 35.
16. *New York Times,* June 16, 1998, p. A1; *ibid.,* June 26, 1998, p. A8.
17. *Newsweek,* Sept. 22, 1997, p. 70.
18. Michael Wilbon, "Now, Jordan Really Means Business," *Washington Post,* Sept. 11, 1997, p. C7.
19. *Fortune,* June 22, 1998, *passim; Washington Post,* June 2, 1998, p. E6.
20. This and the following paragraph are based on Steve Rushin, "World Domination," *Sports Illustrated,* Oct. 27, 1997, pp. 68–71.
21. Alan Freeman, "NBA Drives Growth of Hoops in Germany," *Toronto Globe,* Dec. 23, 1996, p. C11.

22. *New York Times,* Dec. 7, 1997, p. Wk3.

23. *Canadian Business,* 69 (Oct. 1996), p. 113.

24. Richard Pells, *Not Like Us* (New York, 1997), p. 413, also p. 263.

25. *New York Times,* Feb. 26, 1997, p. A23.

26. Orlando Patterson, "Ecumenical America," *World Policy Journal,* 11 (Summer 1994), p. 105.

27. Ronald L. McDonald, *The Complete Hamburger: The History of America's Favorite Sandwich* (Secaucus, N.J., 1997), p. 4. Richard Kuisel, "Not Like Us or More Like Us: America and Europe," *Diplomatic History,* 22 (Fall 1998), p. 620; Richard F. Kuisel, *Seducing the French: The Dilemma of Americanization* (Berkeley, 1993), p. ix.

28. Geoffrey Smith, "The Roar of the Greasepaint, the Smell of the Crowd?" *Queen's Quarterly,* 103 (Fall 1996), pp. 13–15.

29. Wilson Dizard, Jr., *Old Media/New Media: Mass Communications in the Information Age* (New York, 1994), p. 3.

30. *Business Week,* July 29, 1996, pp. 36–37; Rick Reilly, "The Swooshification of the World," *Sports Illustrated,* Feb. 24, 1997, p. 78; Jeff Jensen, "Nike Deals in U.S. . . . ," *Advertising Age,* Oct. 14, 1996, p. 8.

31. Steve Geisi, "Nike Loads U.S. Team . . . ," *Brandweek,* July 17, 1995, p. 12; *Multinational Monitor,* 18 (Dec. 1997), p. 14.

32. *Advertising Age,* Feb. 16, 1998, p. 59.

33. This and the previous paragraph are drawn from *Newsweek,* May 20, 1996, p. 61; *Advertising Age,* Sept. 30, 1996, pp. 2, 62.

34. *Moscow News,* Aug. 14, 1996, p. 9; *Advertising Age,* Dec. 16, 1996, p. 30.

35. *Newsweek,* Oct. 2, 1995, p. 65.

36. *Far Eastern Economic Review,* Aug. 29, 1996, p. 5.

37. This and the following paragraph are drawn from Anne Swardson and Sandra Sugawara, "Asian Workers Become Customers," *Washington Post,* Dec. 30, 1996, p. A16; William Greider, *One World, Ready or Not* (New York, 1997), pp. 390–395, 404; Mark L. Clifford, "Pangs of Conscience," *Business Week,* July 29, 1996, p. 46–47.

38. *Washington Post,* March 28, 1997, p. G2; Bob Herbert, "Brutality in Vietnam," *New York Times,* March 28, 1997, p. A29.

39. *Washington Post,* April 15, 1997, p. A10; *ibid.,* April 10, 1997, p. A19.
40. *New York Times,* June 25, 1997, p. D2; Bob Herbert, "Mr. Young Gets It Wrong," *ibid.,* June 27, 1997, p. A29; *ibid.,* Nov. 8, 1997, p. A1; *Washington Post,* June 28, 1997, p. D1; *Multinational Monitor,* 18 (Dec. 1997), p. 13.
41. *Washington Post,* May 13, 1998, p. C9; *New York Times,* May 13, 1998, p. D1.
42. *Washington Post,* May 13, 1998, p. C9; *New York Times,* May 13, 1998, p. D1.
43. Timothy Egan, "The Swoon of the Swoosh," *New York Times Magazine,* Sept. 13, 1998, pp. 66–70.
44. *Washington Post,* Sept. 9, 1998, p. D1.
45. *Ibid.,* June 16, 1998, p. D3.
46. Harvey Araton, "Athletes Toe the Nike Line . . .," *New York Times,* Nov. 22, 1997, p. C25.
47. *Ibid.*
48. *New York Times,* April 12, 1998, p. 26.
49. Donald Katz, *Just Do It: The Nike Spirit in the Corporate World* (New York, 1994), p. 175.
50. *Economist,* April 11, 1998, p. 39; David Morley and Kevin Robins, *Spaces of Identity: Global Media, Electronic Landscapes, and Cultural Boundaries* (New York, 1995).
51. Joseph S. Nye, Jr., and William A. Owens, "America's Information Edge," *Foreign Affairs,* 75 (March 1996), pp. 29, 35; *Far Eastern Economic Review,* Nov. 20, 1997, pp. 66–67.
52. Richard Sklar, *Postimperialism: Concepts and Implications* (Hanover, N.H., 1997), pp. 22–23.
53. A useful discussion of these points is in John Tomlinson, *Cultural Imperialism: A Critical Introduction* (Baltimore, 1991), esp. pp. 2–5, 19–28.
54. *Chronicle of Higher Education,* March 8, 1998, p. B5.
55. *New York Times,* March 2, 1998, p. D8.
56. Nat Hentoff, "Fred Friendly's Faith in the Constitution," *Washington Post,* March 14, 1998, p. A15.
57. *New York Times,* Aug. 23, 1998, pp. 1, 10.
58. Fouad Ajami, "The Summoning," *Foreign Affairs,* 72 (Sept./Oct. 1993), pp. 2–9.
59. Peter Schwartz and Peter Lyden, "The Long Boom," *Wired,* 5

(July 1997), p. 116; I am indebted to Eric Edelman for this reference.

60. *Economist,* Feb. 1, 1997, p. 18.

61. Masao Miyoshi, " 'Globalization', Culture, and the University," Fredric Jameson and Masao Miyoshi, eds., *The Cultures of Globalization* (Durham, N.C., 1998), p. 259. The post-1880s problem is analyzed, with references, in Walter LaFeber, *The American Search for Opportunity, 1865–1913* (New York, 1993); *New York Times,* Feb. 28, 1998, p. 27.

62. *Economist,* April 11, 1998, p. 39.

63. George Soros, "Toward a Global Open Society," *The Atlantic Monthly,* 281 (Jan. 1998), p. 24.

# Selected Bibliography

On Michael Jordan, the most recent biography is *Michael Jordan: The Making of a Legend,* by David Halberstam (New York, 1999), while Jordan's autobiography is *For the Love of the Game: My Story* (New York, 1998). Excellent earlier biographies and personal accounts of Jordan are Jim Naughton, *Taking to the Air: The Rise of Michael Jordan* (New York, 1992); Bob Greene, *Hang Time: Days and Dreams with Michael Jordan* (New York, 1992); and Greene's follow-up on the retirement and baseball interlude, *Rebound: The Odyssey of Michael Jordan* (New York, 1995). Coach Phil Jackson's revealing memoir, written with Hugh Delehanty, is *Sacred Hoops* (New York, 1995). On Jordan and the Bulls' dynasty, check the footnotes of this book, noting especially Mike Lupica, "Damn Bulls," *Esquire,* 127 (May 1997), and "Bullish on Dynasties," *Washington Post,* June 16, 1998, p. D3.

For the larger sports picture and basketball history, check *Journal of Sport History* and *International Journal of the History of Sport,* as well as the footnotes in this volume. Especially useful are Keith Myerscough, "The Game with No Name: The Invention of Basketball," *International Journal of the History of Sport,* XII (April 1995); Robert W. Peterson, *Cages to Jump Shots: Pro Basketball's Early Years* (New York, 1990); Todd Gould, *Pioneers of the Hardwood* (Bloomington, Ind., 1998), a superbly told story of professional basketball's history in Indiana; anything by

Allen Guttmann, especially *Games and Empires: Modern Sports and Cultural Imperialism* (New York, 1994), and *The Erotic in Sports* (New York, 1996); anything by Randy Roberts, including his and James Olson's *Winning Is the Only Thing: Sports in American Society since 1945* (Baltimore, 1989), notably pp. 114–131, on television in the 1980s; Steven A. Riess's excellent *City Games: The Evolution of American Urban Society and the Rise of Sports* (Urbana, Ill., 1989); an outstanding and important collection of essays (by Elliott Gorn, David K. Wiggins, and Stephen H. Hardy, among others) in S. W. Pope, ed., *The New American Sport History* (Urbana and Chicago, 1997); Susan Cahn, *Coming on Strong* (New York, 1994), for women's sports; Douglas A. Noverr and Lawrence E. Ziewacz, *The Games They Played: Sports in American History, 1865–1980* (Chicago, 1983), highly readable; Robert Lipsyte and Peter Levine, *Idols of the Game: A Sporting History of the American Century* (Atlanta, 1995), important for vivid personality descriptions; Paul D. Staudohar and James A. Mangan, eds., *The Business of Professional Sports* (Urbana, Ill., 1991), an excellent analysis; "Survey: The World of Sport," *Economist,* June 6, 1998, which places U.S. sports in the global context; Arthur Ashe, Jr., *A Hard Road to Glory: A History of the African-American Athlete,* 3 vols. (New York, 1988), an invaluable encyclopedic account by the tennis champion; John Hoberman, *Darwin's Athletes* (Boston, 1997), an incisive analysis of race and racism in sports, especially basketball; and C. L. Cole and D. Andrews, "Look—It's NBA Showtime! Visions of Race in the Popular Imagination," *Cultural Studies, Annual I* (1995).

On the transnational corporations, note, in addition to this book's footnotes, the columns in *Advertising Age, Multinational Monitor,* and *Brandweek,* especially important for marketing and public relations. The historical background is superbly presented in Mira Wilkins, *The Emergence of Multinational Enterprise: American Business Abroad from the Colonial Era to 1914* (Cambridge, Mass., 1970); and Richard Barnet and Ronald E. Muller, *Global Reach: The Power of the Multinational Corporations* (New York, 1974). For the new transnationals, note especially Richard J. Barnet and John Cavanagh, *Global Dreams: Imperial Corporations and the New World Order* (New York, 1994); Peter F. Drucker, *Post-Capitalist Society* (New York, 1993), written by the dean of corporate studies; William Greider, *One World, Ready or Not: The Manic Logic of Global Capitalism* (New York, 1997), a sharply critical analysis; the review of Greider's book by Dwight D. Murphey, "Reflections on Global Capitalism," in *Journal of Social, Political and Economic Studies,* 21 (Winter 1997); and John Cassidy, "The Next Thinker: The Return of Karl Marx," *New Yorker,* Oct. 20 and 27, 1997.

On globalization, Americanization, and the media, especially as they relate to sports, check the footnotes in this book as well as Jean Harvey and François Houle, "Sport, World Economy, Global Culture, and New Social Movements," *Sociology of Sport Journal,* 11 (Dec. 1994), a valuable overview; Roland Robertson, "Mapping the Global Condition: Globalization as the Central Concept," *Theory, Culture and Society,* 7 (June 1990); Fredric Jameson and Masao Miyoshi, eds., *The Cultures of Globalization* (Durham, N.C, 1998), especially Jameson's Preface, and essays by Myoshi, Hettata, and Sklar; John Tomlinson, *Cultural Imperialism: A Critical Introduction* (Baltimore, 1991), by a scholar who, like Robertson, is pivotal in the field; James Petras, "Culture Imperialism in the Late 20th Century," *Journal of Contemporary Asia,* 23 (no. 2, 1993); Martin Albrow, *The Global Age: State and Society Beyond Modernity* (Cambridge, U.K., 1996); Richard Kuisel, *Seducing the French: The Dilemma of Americanization* (Berkeley, 1993), especially valuable; Richard Pells, *Not Like Us: How Europeans Have Loved, Hated, and Transformed American Culture since World War II* (New York, 1997), a pioneering account that somewhat differs from Kuisel's emphases; Roger Rollin, ed., *The Americanization of the Global Village: Essays in Comparative Popular Culture* (Bowling Green, Ohio, 1989); Rob Kroes, Robert W. Rydell, and Doeko F. J. Bosscher, eds., *Cultural Transmissions and Receptions: American Mass Culture in Europe* (Amsterdam, 1993), especially the Kroes and Palmié, and Pells and Gilbert essays. The rises and declines of Nike can be traced in Donald Katz, *Just Do It: The Nike Spirit in the Corporate World* (New York, 1994), highly useful; and Timothy Egan, "The Swoon of the Swoosh," *New York Times Magazine,* Sept. 13, 1998. On the media, note "Survey: Telecommunications," *Economist,* Oct. 23, 1993; Marshall McLuhan, *Understanding Media: The Extensions of Man,* 2nd ed. (New York, 1964), by the guru of the new media age; Daniel J. Czitrom, *Media and the American Mind: From Morse to McLuhan* (Chapel Hill, 1982), important historical context; James Lull, *Media, Communication, Culture: A Global Approach* (New York, 1995), valuable for its theoretical framework and comments on "imperialism"; Ken Auletta, *The Highwaymen: Warriors of the Information Superhighway* (New York, 1997), important on the subject as is anything Auletta writes; Greg MacDonald, *The Emergence of Global Multi-Media Conglomerates* (Geneva, 1990); Herbert Schiller, "Not Yet the Post-Imperialist Era," *Critical Studies in Mass Communications,* 8 (March 1991), by a widely noted scholar; William Shawcross, *Murdoch* (New York, 1993), the most recent biography, but also see *New York Times,* March 8, 1998, p. 1, for a listing of the Murdoch empire and especially the links with sports; Robert Goldberg and Gerald Jay Goldberg, *Citizen Turner: The Wild Rise of an American Tycoon* (New York, 1995), entertaining and the only detailed biography. For a highly readable overview of the 1960s–1970s consumer revolution, enjoy Thomas Frank, *The Conquest of Cool* (Chicago, 1997).

# Index